The Spokesman
From Tom Paine to Guantanamo
Edited by Ken Coates
Published by Spokesman for the
Bertrand Russell Peace Foundation

Spokesman 83   2004

CONTENTS

Editorial	3	Ken Coates
Broad Daylight	5	James Kirkup
Iraq Implodes	7	Robert Fisk
Living with Fahrenheit 9/11	10	Michael Moore
Thomas Paine	14	Bertrand Russell
Skull and Bones	23	Kurt Vonnegut
Torture is a Crime	26	Inge Genefke & Bent Sørenson

European Social Forum in London

Another World Is Possible	33	Ken Coates
Charter of Principles	38	World Social Forum
The Europe We Need	41	Robin Blackburn
The Social State in Europe	50	André Brie MEP
Empire in Africa	62	Michael Barratt Brown
Peace Dossier	67	Detention in Afghanistan & Guantanamo Bay: Statement of Shafiq Rasul, Asif Iqbal & Rhuhel Ahmed Health and Human Rights Boston Social Forum World Tribunal on Iraq Israel's Illegal Wall Russell on Radio Wins Award Afghanistan: The Subversion of Relief Hiroshima's Peace Declaration
Reviews	90	Rosemary Thomas Tony Simpson Ken Fleet Michael Barratt Brown

Subscriptions
Institutions £30.00/€60/$60
Individuals £20.00 (UK)
                £25.00 (ex UK)
                €40/$40

Back issues available on request

A CIP catalogue record for this book is available from the British Library

Published by the
Bertrand Russell Peace Foundation Ltd.,
Russell House
Bulwell Lane
Nottingham NG6 0BT
England
Tel. 0115 9784504
email:
elfeuro@compuserve.com
www.spokesmanbooks.com
www.russfound.org

Editorial Board:
Michael Barratt Brown
Ken Coates
John Daniels
Ken Fleet
Stuart Holland
Tony Simpson

the union

Amicus fighting for the liberty of working people at home and abroad

General Secretary
Derek Simpson

Editorial

From Tom Paine to Guantanamo

As Bertrand Russell pointed out, at a time when Tom Paine was less popular than he is today, his importance in history

> 'consists in the fact that he made the preaching of democracy democratic. There were, in the eighteenth century, democrats among French and English aristocrats, among *philosophes* and Nonconformist ministers. But all of them presented their political speculations in a form designed to appeal only to the educated. Paine, while his doctrine contained nothing novel, was an innovator in the manner of his writing, which was simple, direct, unlearned and such as every intelligent working man could appreciate. This made him dangerous...'

'It was' wrote Russell, 'his fate to be honoured by oppositions and hated by governments'. Much the same thing could be said of Russell himself, who, like Paine, lived through cycles of official approval and contempt. *Rights of Man* was initially dedicated to George Washington, that they

> 'may become as universal as your Benevolence can wish, and that you may enjoy the Happiness of seeing the New World regenerate the Old'.

But Washington did not wish for such regeneration and was distinctly suspicious of the establishment of human rights in France, even before the revolution plunged into bloodshed. When Paine himself was in danger of execution, Washington did nothing to save him, and indeed Robespierre, publishing an accusation against Paine, did so 'for the interest of America as well as of France'.

Enfeebled by the illness he developed in a French prison, Paine wrote to Washington on his release, to say that whether he recovered from his illness or not

> 'I shall continue to think you treacherous, till you give me cause to think otherwise. I am sure you would have found yourself more at your ease, had you acted by me as you ought; for whether your desertion of me was intended to gratify the English Government, or to let me fall into destruction in France, that you might exclaim the louder against the French revolution; or whether you hoped by my extinction to meet with less opposition in mounting up the American Government; either of these will involve you in reproach you will not easily shake off.'

As Russell rightly says, Paine had his faults, like other men; 'but it was for his virtues that he was hated and successfully calumniated'.

Today the United States, thanks in no small part to the legacy of Tom Paine, is truly a territory of vast importance for liberty and civil freedom. But these virtues are less and less celebrated because a suspicious world, with equal justice, finds them less and less credible. In an age of brutal imperial wars, shock and awe, and scientific industrial butchery, it becomes more and more difficult to believe in America's fidelity to original revolutionary principles and human rights. Now, at a culminating point in the slaughter in Iraq, we have the exposure of torture in the prison at Abu Ghraib, and the unmasking of the systematic cruelties of the detention centre at Guantanamo Bay. We republish below a small part of the compelling testimony of Shafiq Rasul, Asif Iqbal and Rhuhel Ahmed who were freighted with other victims from captivity in Afghanistan, after enduring brutal interrogations, to prison planes bound for Cuba. Their captors were quick to inform them that since no one knew where they were, anything could be done to them without arousing any complaint. In the prisons of the British Empire, or of the French terror, there was brutality enough: but in these modernising American prisons brutality is combined with exquisite mental torture, aimed at the extinction of the last residue of hope from those it entraps.

All this is dominance, for sure: a small fraction of that Full Spectrum Dominance which animates military doctrine in the world's only megapower. This proclaims the intention of ruling the earth, air, seas and space, as well as information. It does not proclaim its equally depraved intention of extinguishing alternative hopes and limiting all licence for the imagination, or any spark of creativity which is not securely commercial.

We have for a long time warned that Full Spectrum Dominance is not a very rational objective. Today may be discerned, if but faintly, the writing which has appeared on the wall. We do not refer to the slogans which we have written there, echoing Tom Paine, for human rights. No, today's faint writing may be seen in the financial newspapers in analyses of the current account deficit of the United States, and in forecasts which anticipate, according to Wynne Godley, 'a fiscal deficit…{climbing towards}…nine per cent of GDP four or so years from now'. Martin Wolf, writing in the *Financial Times*, gives his judgement:

> 'Let us be blunt about it. The US is now on the comfortable path to ruin. It is being driven along a road of ever rising deficits and debt, both external and fiscal, that risk destroying the country's credit and the global role of its currency. It is also, not coincidentally, likely to generate an unmanageable increase in US protectionism'.

Within ten years, thinks Wolf, the US 'will have lost control over its economic fate'.

Of course, this may never happen. Contemplating it may compel the invention of other options. The great Russian military Moloch perished because it ate more resources than its society could engender. We may be some time away from the similar implosion of Full Spectrum Dominance, and it is always possible that it may destroy large parts of the world before its account is settled. But there was a reason why the military planners did not proclaim Full Spectrum Dominance of hope. This human dimension is ultimately beyond the reach of the generals, and even of the Presidents.

Ken Coates

BROAD DAYLIGHT

(on not understanding, which is Zen)

Out of all the world
take this forest.

Out of all the forest
take this tree.

Out of all the tree
take this branch.

Out of all the branch
take this leaf.

And on this leaf
that is like no other

observe this drop of rain
that is like no other.

And in this single drop
observe the reflection

of leaves and branches,
of the entire tree,

of the forest,
of all the world –

Then only
will you see

the stars beyond
the light of day.

James Kirkup

No More Hiroshimas, Poems and Translations by James Kirkup, is newly published by Spokesman Books (£6.99).

Routledge Classics

Get inside one of the greatest minds of the 20th Century

Six Bertrand Russell titles

'There is no one who uses the English language more beguilingly than Russell, no one smoothes the kinks and creases more artfully out of the most crumpled weaves of thought.' - *The Times*

Prices from £7.99 to £12.99

Available from all good bookshops or visit www.routledgeclassics.com

Also published in Routledge Classics...

Adorno ... Andersen ... Barth ... Blake ... Bohm ... Buber ... Derrida ... Durkheim ... Eagleton
Einstein ... Foucault ... Freud ... Fromm ... Grimm ... Hayek ... Jameson ... Jung ... Kermode ... Lacan
Lear ... Lévi-Strauss ... Lorenz ... McLuhan ... Marcuse ... Mauss ... Merleau-Ponty ... Midgley
Murdoch ... Piaget ... Popper ... Ricoeur ... Sartre ... Weber ... Weil ... Wittgenstein ... Yeats

More than 100 titles available

Iraq Implodes

Robert Fisk

'*Doesn't Blair realise that Iraq is about to implode?*' Robert Fisk is the Middle East correspondent of the London Independent. *His new book,* The Great War for Civilisation: The Conquest of the Middle East, *will be published later this year.*

The war is a fraud. I'm not talking about the weapons of mass destruction that didn't exist. Nor the links between Saddam Hussein and al-Qa'ida which didn't exist. Nor all the other lies upon which we went to war. I'm talking about the new lies.

For just as, before the war, our governments warned us of threats that did not exist; now they hide from us the threats that do exist. Much of Iraq has fallen outside the control of America's puppet government in Baghdad but we are not told. Hundreds of attacks are made against US troops every month. But unless an American dies, we are not told. This month's death toll of Iraqis in Baghdad alone has now reached 700 – the worst month since the invasion ended. But we are not told.

The stage management of this catastrophe in Iraq was all too evident at Saddam Hussein's 'trial'. Not only did the US military censor the tapes of the event. Not only did they effectively delete all sound of the 11 other defendants. But the Americans led Saddam Hussein to believe – until he reached the courtroom – that he was on his way to his execution. Indeed, when he entered the room he believed that the judge was there to condemn him to death. This, after all, was the way Saddam ran his own state security courts. No wonder he initially looked 'disorientated' – CNN's helpful description – because, of course, he was meant to look that way. We had made sure of that. Which is why Saddam asked Judge Juhi: 'Are you a lawyer?. ..Is this a trial?' And swiftly, as he realised that this really was an initial court hearing – not a preliminary to his own hanging – he quickly adopted an attitude of belligerence.

But don't think we're going to learn much more about Saddam's future court appearances. Salem Chalabi, the brother of convicted fraudster Ahmad and the man entrusted by the Americans with the tribunal, told the Iraqi press two weeks ago that all media would be excluded from future court hearings. And I can see why. Because if Saddam does a Milosevic, he'll want to talk about the real intelligence and military connections of his regime – which were primarily with the United States.

Living in Iraq these past few weeks is a weird as well as dangerous experience. I drive down to Najaf. Highway 8 is one of the worst in Iraq. Westerners are murdered there. It is littered with burnt-out police vehicles and American trucks. Every police post for 70 miles has been abandoned. Yet a few hours later, I am sitting in my room in Baghdad watching Tony Blair, grinning in the House of Commons as if he is the hero of a school debating competition; so much for the Butler report.

Indeed, watching any Western television station in Baghdad these days is like tuning in to Planet Mars. Doesn't Blair realise that Iraq is about to implode? Doesn't Bush realise this? The American-appointed 'government' controls only parts of Baghdad – and even there its ministers and civil servants are car-bombed and assassinated. Baquba, Samara, Kut, Mahmoudiya, Hilla, Fallujah, Ramadi, all are outside government authority. Iyad Allawi, the 'Prime Minister', is little more than mayor of Baghdad. 'Some journalists,' Blair announces, 'almost want there to be a disaster in Iraq.' He doesn't get it. The disaster exists now.

When suicide bombers ram their cars into hundreds of recruits outside police stations, how on earth can anyone hold an election next January? Even the National Conference to appoint those who will arrange elections has been twice postponed. And looking back through my notebooks over the past five weeks, I find that not a single Iraqi, not a single American soldier I have spoken to, not a single mercenary – be he American, British or South African – believes that there will be elections in January. All said that Iraq is deteriorating by the day. And most asked why we journalists weren't saying so.

But in Baghdad, I turn on my television and watch Bush telling his Republican supporters that Iraq is improving, that Iraqis support the 'coalition', that they support their new US-manufactured government, that the 'war on terror' is being won, that Americans are safer. Then I go to an internet site and watch two hooded men hacking off the head of an American in Riyadh, tearing at the vertebrae of an American in Iraq with a knife. Each day, the papers here list another construction company pulling out of the country. And I go down to visit the friendly, tragically sad staff of the Baghdad mortuary and there, each day, are dozens of those Iraqis we supposedly came to liberate, screaming and weeping and cursing as they carry their loved ones on their shoulders in cheap coffins.

I keep re-reading Tony Blair's statement. 'I remain convinced it was right to go to war. It was the most difficult decision of my life.' And I cannot understand it. It may be a terrible decision to go to war. Even Chamberlain thought that; but he didn't find it a difficult decision – because, after the Nazi invasion of Poland, it was the right thing to do. And driving the streets of Baghdad now, watching the terrified American patrols, hearing yet another thunderous explosion shaking my windows and doors after dawn, I realise what all this means. Going to war in Iraq, invading Iraq last year was the most difficult decision Blair had to take because he thought – correctly – that it might be the wrong decision. I will always remember his remark to British troops in Basra, that the sacrifice of British soldiers was not Hollywood but 'real flesh and blood'. Yes, it was real flesh and blood that was shed – but for weapons of mass destruction that weren't real at all.

'Deadly force is authorised,' it says on checkpoints all over Baghdad. Authorised by whom? There is no accountability. Repeatedly, on the great highways out of the city US soldiers shriek at motorists and open fire at the least suspicion. 'We had some Navy Seals down at our checkpoint the other day,' a 1st Cavalry sergeant says to me. 'They asked if we were having any trouble. I said, yes, they've been shooting at us from a house over there. One of them asked: "That house?" We said yes. So they have these three SUVs and a lot of weapons made of titanium and they drive off towards the house. And later they come back and say "We've taken care of that". And we didn't get shot at any more.'

What does this mean? The Americans are now bragging about their siege of Najaf. Lieutenant Colonel Garry Bishop of the 37th Armoured Division's 1st Battalion believes it was an 'ideal' battle (even though he failed to kill or capture Muqtada Sadr whose 'Mehdi army' were fighting the US forces). It was 'ideal', Bishop explained, because the Americans avoided damaging the holy shrines of the Imams Ali and Hussein. What are Iraqis to make of this? What if a Muslim army occupied Kent and bombarded Canterbury and then bragged that they hadn't damaged Canterbury Cathedral? Would we be grateful?

What, indeed, are we to make of a war which is turned into a fantasy by those who started it? As foreign workers pour out of Iraq for fear of their lives, US Secretary of State Colin Powell tells a press conference that hostage taking is having an 'effect' on reconstruction. Effect! Oil pipeline explosions are now as regular as power cuts. In parts of Baghdad now, they have only four hours of electricity a day; the streets swarm with foreign mercenaries, guns poking from windows, shouting abusively at Iraqis who don't clear the way for them. This is the 'safer' Iraq, which Mr Blair was boasting of the other day. What world does the British Government exist in?

Take the Saddam trial. The entire Arab press – including the Baghdad papers – prints the judge's name. Indeed, the same judge has given interviews about his charges of murder against Muqtada Sadr. He has posed for newspaper pictures. But when I mention his name in *The Independent*, I was solemnly censured by the British Government's spokesman. Salem Chalabi threatened to prosecute me. So let me get this right. We illegally invade Iraq. We kill up to 11,000 Iraqis. And Mr Chalabi, appointed by the Americans, says I'm guilty of 'incitement to murder'. That just about says it all.

©Robert Fisk, *The Independent*. This article first appeared in *The Independent on Sunday* 1st August 2004.

Living with Fahrenheit 9/11

Michael Moore

Friends,

Where do I begin? This past week has knocked me for a loop. 'Fahrenheit 9/11,' the No. 1 movie in the country, the largest grossing documentary ever. My head is spinning. Didn't we just lose our distributor eight weeks ago? Did Karl Rove really fail to stop this? Is Bush packing?

Each day this week I was given a new piece of information from the press that covers Hollywood, and I barely had time to recover from the last titbit before the next one smacked me upside the head

- More people saw 'Fahrenheit 9/11' in one weekend than all the people who saw 'Bowling for Columbine' in 9 months.
- 'Fahrenheit 9/11' broke 'Rocky III's' record for the biggest box office opening weekend ever for any film that opened in less than a thousand theatres.
- 'Fahrenheit 9/11' beat the opening weekend of 'Return of the Jedi.'
- 'Fahrenheit 9/11' instantly went to No. 2 on the all-time list for largest per-theatre average ever for a film that opened in wide-release.

How can I ever thank all of you who went to see it?

These records are mind-blowing. They have sent shock waves through Hollywood – and, more importantly, through the White House.

But it didn't just stop there. The response to the movie then went into the Twilight Zone. Surfing through the dial I landed on the Fox broadcasting network which was airing the NASCAR race live last Sunday to an audience of millions of Americans – and suddenly the announcers were talking about how NASCAR champ Dale Earnhardt, Jr. took his crew to see 'Fahrenheit 9/11' the night before. FOX sportscaster Chris Myers delivered Earnhardt's review straight out of his mouth and into the heartland of America: 'He said hey, it'll be a good bonding experience no matter what your political belief. It's a good thing as an American to go see.' Whoa! NASCAR fans – you can't go

The film-maker Michael Moore is author of Dude, Where's My Country? *and* Stupid White Men... And Other Sorry Excuses for the State of the Nation!

deeper into George Bush territory than that! White House moving vans – START YOUR ENGINES!

Then there was Roger Friedman from the Fox News Channel giving our film an absolutely glowing review, calling it 'a really brilliant piece of work, and a film that members of all political parties should see without fail.' Richard Goldstein of the *Village Voice* surmised that Bush is already considered a goner so Rupert Murdoch might be starting to curry favor with the new administration. I don't know about that, but I've never heard a decent word toward me from Fox. So, after I was revived, I wondered if a love note to me from Sean Hannity was next.

How about Letterman's Top Ten List: 'Top Ten George W. Bush Complaints About 'Fahrenheit 9/11':

10. That actor who played the President was totally unconvincing
9. It oversimplified the way I stole the election
8. Too many of them fancy college-boy words
7. If Michael Moore had waited a few months, he could have included the part where I get him deported
6. Didn't have one of them hilarious monkeys who smoke cigarettes and gives people the finger
5. Of all Michael Moore's accusations, only 97% are true
4. Not sure – I passed out after a piece of popcorn lodged in my windpipe
3. Where the hell was Spider-man?
2. Couldn't hear most of the movie over Cheney's foul mouth
1. I thought this was supposed to be about dodgeball

But it was the reactions and reports we received from theatres around the country that really sent me over the edge. One theatre manager after another phoned in to say that the movie was getting standing ovations as the credits rolled – in places like Greensboro, NC and Oklahoma City – and that they were having a hard time clearing the theatre afterwards because people were either too stunned or they wanted to sit and talk to their neighbours about what they had just seen. In Trumbull, CT, one woman got up on her seat after the movie and shouted 'Let's go have a meeting!' A man in San Francisco took his shoe off and threw it at the screen when Bush appeared at the end. Ladies' church groups in Tulsa were going to see it, and weeping afterwards.

It was this last group that gave lie to all the yakking pundits who, before the movie opened, declared that only the hard-core 'choir' would go to see 'Fahrenheit 9/11.' They couldn't have been more wrong. Theatres in the Deep South and the Midwest set house records for any film they'd ever shown. Yes, it even sold out in Peoria. And Lubbock, Texas. And Anchorage, Alaska!

Newspaper after newspaper wrote stories in tones of breathless disbelief about people who called themselves 'Independents' and 'Republicans' walking out of the movie theatre shaken and in tears, proclaiming that they could not, in good conscience, vote for George W. Bush. *The New York Times* wrote of a conservative Republican woman in her 20s in Pensacola, Florida who cried through the film, and told the reporter: 'It really makes me question what I feel about the President...it makes me question his motives'

Newsday reported on a self-described 'ardent Bush/Cheney supporter' who went to see the film on Long Island, and his quiet reaction afterwards. He said, 'It's really given me pause to think about what's really going on. There was just too much – too much to discount.' The man then bought three more tickets for another showing of the film.

The *Los Angeles Times* found a mother who had 'supported [Bush] fiercely' at a theatre in Des Peres, Missouri: 'Emerging from Michael Moore's Fahrenheit 9/11, her eyes wet, Leslie Hanser said she at last understood. "My emotions are just..." She trailed off, waving her hands to show confusion. "I feel like we haven't seen the whole truth before."'

All of this had to be the absolute worst news for the White House to wake up to on Monday morning. I guess they were in such a stupor, they 'gave' Iraq back to, um, Iraq two days early!

News editors told us that they were being 'bombarded' with e-mails and calls from the White House (read: Karl Rove), trying to spin their way out of this mess by attacking it and attacking me. Bush spokesman Dan Bartlett had told the White House press corps that the movie was 'outrageously false' – even though he said he hadn't seen the movie. He later told CNN that 'This is a film that doesn't require us to actually view it to know that it's filled with factual inaccuracies.' At least they're consistent. They never needed to see a single weapon of mass destruction before sending our kids off to die.

Many news shows were more than eager to buy the White House spin. After all, that is a big part of what 'Fahrenheit' is about – how the lazy, compliant media bought all the lies from the Bush administration about the need to invade Iraq. They took the Kool-Aid offered by the White House and rarely, if ever, did our media ask the hard questions that needed to be asked before the war started.

Because the movie 'outs' the mainstream media for their failures and their complicity with the Bush administration – who can ever forget their incessant, embarrassing cheerleading as the troops went off to war, as though it was all just a game – the media was not about to let me get away with anything now resembling a cultural phenomenon. On show after show, they went after me with the kind of viciousness you would have hoped they had had for those who were lying about the necessity for invading a sovereign nation that was no threat to us. I don't blame our well-paid celebrity journalists – they look like a bunch of ass-kissing dopes in my movie, and I guess I'd be pretty mad at me, too. After all, once the NASCAR fans see 'Fahrenheit 9/11,' will they ever believe a single thing they see on ABC/NBC/CBS news again?

In the next week or so, I will recount my adventures through the media this past month (I will also be posting a full FAQ on my website soon so that you can have all the necessary backup and evidence from the film when you find yourself in heated debate with your conservative brother-in-law!). For now, please know the following: Every single fact I state in 'Fahrenheit 9/11' is the absolute and irrefutable truth. This movie is perhaps the most thoroughly researched and vetted documentary of our time. No fewer than a dozen people, including three teams of lawyers and the venerable one-time fact-checkers from *The New Yorker* went through this movie with a fine-tooth comb so that we can make this guarantee to you. Do not let anyone say this or that isn't true. If they say that, they are lying. Let them know that the OPINIONS in the film are mine, and anyone certainly has a right to disagree with them. And the questions I pose in the movie, based on these irrefutable facts, are also mine. And I have a right to ask them. And I will continue to ask them until they are answered.

In closing, let me say that the most heartening response to the film has come from our soldiers and their families. Theatres in military towns across the country reported packed houses. Our troops know the truth. They have seen it first-hand. And many of them could not believe that here was a movie that was TRULY on their side – the side of bringing them home alive and never sending them into harm's way again unless it's the absolute last resort. Please take a moment to read this wonderful story from the daily paper in Fayetteville, NC, where Fort Bragg is located. It broke my heart to read this, the reactions of military families and the comments of an infantryman's wife publicly backing my movie – and it gave me the resolve to make sure as many Americans as possible see this film in the coming weeks.

Thank you again, all of you, for your support. Together we did something for the history books. My apologies to 'Return of the Jedi.' We'll make it up by producing 'Return of the Texan to Crawford' in November.

May the farce be with you, but not for long.

©*Michael Moore* www.michaelmoore.com mmflint@aol.com

P.S. You can read letters from people around the country recounting their own experiences at the theatre, and their reactions to the film by going here.
P.P.S. Also, I'm going to start blogging! Tonight! Come on over and check it out.

Thomas Paine
1739-1809

Bertrand Russell

'Paine's importance in history consists in the fact that he made the preaching of democracy democratic.' Russell's essay on Tom Paine was first published in 1934.

Thomas Paine, though prominent in two Revolutions and almost hanged for attempting to raise a third, is grown, in our day, somewhat dim. To our great-grandfathers, he seemed a kind of earthly Satan, a subversive infidel rebellious alike against his God and his King. He incurred the bitter hostility of three men not generally united: Pitt, Robespierre, and Washington. Of these the first two sought his death, while the third carefully abstained from measures designed to save his life. Pitt and Washington hated him because he was a democrat; Robespierre, because he opposed the execution of the King and the Reign of Terror. It was his fate to be always honoured by Oppositions and hated by Governments: Washington, while he was still fighting the English, spoke of Paine in terms of the highest praise; the French nation heaped honours upon him until the Jacobins rose to power; even in England, the most prominent Whig statesmen befriended him and employed him in drawing up manifestos. He had faults, like other men; but it was for his virtues that he was hated and successfully calumniated.

Paine's importance in history consists in the fact that he made the preaching of democracy democratic. There were, in the eighteenth century, democrats among French and English aristocrats, among *philosophes* and Nonconformist ministers. But all of them presented their political speculations in a form designed to appeal only to the educated. Paine, while his doctrine contained nothing novel, was an innovator in the manner of his writing, which was simple, direct, unlearned, and such as every intelligent working man could appreciate. This made him dangerous; and when he added religious unorthodoxy to his other crimes, the defenders of privilege seized the opportunity to load him with obloquy.

The first thirty-six years of his life gave no evidence of the talents which appeared in his later activities. He was born at Thetford, in

1739, of poor Quaker parents, and was educated at the local grammar school up to the age of thirteen, when he became a stay-maker. A quiet life, however, was not his taste, and at the age of seventeen he tried to enlist on a privateer called *The Terrible,* whose Captain's name was Death. His parents fetched him back, and so probably saved his life, as 175 out of the crew of 200 were shortly afterwards killed in action. A little later, however, on the outbreak of the Seven Years' War, he succeeded in sailing on another privateer, but nothing is known of his brief adventures at sea. In 1758, he was employed as a stay-maker in London, and in the following year he married, but his wife died after a few months. In 1763 he became an exciseman, but was dismissed two years later for professing to have made inspections while he was in fact studying at home. In great poverty, he became a schoolmaster at ten shillings a week, and tried to take Anglican orders. From such desperate expedients he was saved by being reinstated as an exciseman at Lewes, where he married a Quakeress from whom, for reasons unknown, he formally separated in 1774. In this year he again lost his employment, apparently because he organised a petition of the excisemen for higher pay. By selling all that he had, he was just able to pay his debts and leave some provision for his wife, but he himself was again reduced to destitution.

In London, where he was trying to present the excisemen's petition to Parliament, he made the acquaintance of Benjamin Franklin, who thought well of him. The result was that, in October 1774, he sailed for America, armed with a letter of recommendation from Franklin describing him as an 'ingenious, worthy young man.' As soon as he arrived in Philadelphia, he began to show skill as a writer, and almost immediately became editor of a journal.

His first publication, in March 1775, was a forcible article against slavery and the slave trade, to which, whatever some of his American friends might say, he remained always an uncompromising enemy. It seems to have been largely owing to his influence that Jefferson inserted in the draft of the Declaration of Independence the passage on this subject which was afterwards cut out. In 1775, slavery still existed in Pennsylvania; it was abolished in that State by an Act of 1780, of which, it was generally believed, Paine wrote the preamble.

Paine was one of the first, if not the very first, to advocate complete freedom for the United States. In October, 1775, when even those who subsequently signed the Declaration of Independence were still hoping for some accommodation with the British Government, he wrote:

> 'I hesitate not for a moment to believe that the Almighty will finally separate America from Britain. Call it Independency or what you will, if it is the cause of God and humanity it will go on. And when the Almighty shall have blest us, and made us a people *dependent only upon him,* then may our first gratitude be shown by an act of continental legislation, which shall put a stop to the importation of Negroes for sale, soften the hard fate of those already here, and in time procure their freedom.'

It was for the sake of freedom – freedom from monarchy, aristocracy, slavery, and every species of tyranny – that Paine took up the cause of America.

During the most difficult years of the War of Independence he spent his days campaigning and his evenings composing rousing manifestos published under the signature 'Common Sense.' These had enormous success, and helped materially in winning the war. After the British had burnt the towns of Falmouth in Maine and Norfolk in Virginia, Washington wrote to a friend (January 31st, 1776):

> 'A few more of such flaming arguments as were exhibited at Falmouth and Norfolk, added to the sound doctrine and unanswerable reasoning contained in the pamphlet *Common Sense,* will not leave numbers at a loss to decide upon the propriety of separation.'

The work was topical, and has now only a historical interest, but there are phrases in it that are still telling. After pointing out that the quarrel is not only with the King, but also with Parliament, he says: 'There is no body of men more jealous of their privileges than the Commons: Because they sell them.' At that date it was impossible to deny the justice of this taunt.

There is vigorous argument in favour of a Republic, and a triumphant refutation of the theory that monarchy prevents civil war. 'Monarchy and succession,' he says, after a summary of English history, 'have laid...the world in blood and ashes. 'Tis a form of government which the word of God bears testimony against, and blood will attend it.' In December, 1776, at a moment when the fortunes of war were adverse, Paine published a pamphlet called *The Crisis,* beginning:

> 'These are the times that try men's souls. The summer soldier and the sunshine patriot will, in this crisis, shrink from the service of their country; but he that stands it *now* deserves the love and thanks of man and woman.'

This essay was read to the troops, and Washington expressed to Paine a 'living sense of the importance of your works'. No other writer was so widely read in America, and he could have made large sums by his pen, but he always refused to accept any money at all for what he wrote. At the end of the War of Independence, he was universally respected in the United States, but still poor; however, one State legislature voted him a sum of money and another gave him an estate, so that he had every prospect of comfort for the rest of his life. He might have been expected to settle down into the respectability characteristic of revolutionaries who have succeeded. He turned his attention from politics to engineering, and demonstrated the possibility of iron bridges with longer spans than had previously been thought feasible. Iron bridges led him to England, where he was received in a friendly manner by Burke, the Duke of Portland, and other Whig notables. He had a large model of his iron bridge set up at Paddington; he was praised by eminent engineers, and seemed likely to spend his remaining years as an inventor.

However, France as well as England was interested in iron bridges. In 1788 he paid a visit to Paris to discuss them with Lafayette, and to submit his plans to the

Académie des Sciences, which, after due delay, reported favourably. When the Bastille fell, Lafayette decided to present the key of the prison to Washington, and entrusted to Paine the task of conveying it across the Atlantic. Paine, however, was kept in Europe by the affairs of his bridge. He wrote a long letter to Washington informing him that he would find some one to take his place in transporting 'this early trophy of the spoils of despotism, and the first ripe fruits of American principles transplanted into Europe.' He goes on to say that 'I have not the least doubt of the final and compleat success of the French Revolution,' and that 'I have manufactured a Bridge (a single arch) of one hundred and ten feet span, and five feet high from the cord of the arch.'

For a time, the bridge and the Revolution remained thus evenly balanced in his interests, but gradually the Revolution conquered. In the hope of rousing a responsive movement in England, he wrote his *Rights of Man*, on which his fame as a democrat chiefly rests.

This work, which was considered madly subversive during the anti-Jacobin reaction, will astonish a modern reader by its mildness and common sense. It is, primarily, an answer to Burke, and deals at considerable length with contemporary events in France. The first part was published in 1791, the second in 1792; there was, therefore, as yet no need to apologise for the Revolution. There is very little declamation about Natural Rights, but a great deal of sound sense about the British Government. Burke had contended that the Revolution in 1688 bound the British forever to submit to the sovereigns appointed by the Act of Settlement. Paine contends that it is impossible to bind posterity, and that constitutions must be capable of revision from time to time.

Governments, he says, 'may all be comprehended under three heads. First, Superstition. Secondly, Power. Thirdly, The common interest of society and the common rights of man. The first was a government of priestcraft, the second of conquerors, the third of reason.' The two former amalgamated: 'the key of St. Peter and the key of the Treasury became quartered on one another, and the wondering, cheated multitude worshipped the invention.' Such general observations, however, are rare. The bulk of the work consists, first, of French history from 1789 to the end of 1791, and secondly, of a comparison of the British Constitution with that decreed in France in 1791, of course to the advantage of the latter. It must be remembered that in 1791 France was still a monarchy. Paine was a republican and did not conceal the fact, but did not much emphasise it in *Rights of Man*.

Paine's appeal, except in a few short passages, was to common sense. He argued against Pitt's finance, as Cobbett did later, on grounds which ought to have appealed to any Chancellor of the Exchequer; he described the combination of a small sinking fund with vast borrowings as setting a man with a wooden leg to catch a hare – the longer they run, the further apart they are. He speaks of the 'Potter's field of paper money' – a phrase quite in Cobbett's style. It was, in fact, his writings on finance that turned Cobbett's former enmity into admiration. His objection to the hereditary principle, which horrified Burke and Pitt, is now common ground among all politicians, including even Mussolini and Hitler. Nor is his style in any way outrageous: it is clear, vigorous, and downright, but not nearly as abusive as that of his opponents.

Nevertheless, Pitt decided to inaugurate his reign of terror by prosecuting Paine and suppressing *Rights of Man*. According to his niece, Lady Hester Stanhope, he 'used to say that Tom Paine was quite in the right, but then, he would add, what am I to do? As things are, if I were to encourage Tom Paine's opinions we should have a bloody revolution.' Paine replied to the prosecution by defiance and inflammatory speeches. But the September massacres were occurring, and English Tories were reacting by increased fierceness. The poet Blake – who had more worldly wisdom than Paine – persuaded him that if he stayed in England he would be hanged. He fled to France, missing the officers, who had come to arrest him, by a few hours in London and by twenty minutes in Dover, where he was allowed by the authorities to pass because he happened to have with him a recent friendly letter from Washington.

Although England and France were not yet at war, Dover and Calais belonged to different worlds. Paine, who had been elected an honorary French citizen, had been returned to the Convention by three different constituencies, of which Calais, which now welcomed him, was one. 'As the packet sails in a salute is fired from the battery; cheers sound along the shore. As the representative for Calais steps on French soil soldiers make his avenue, the officers embrace him, the national cockade is presented' – and so on, through the usual French series of beautiful ladies, mayors, etc.

Arrived in Paris, he behaved with more public spirit than prudence. He hoped – in spite of the massacres – for an orderly and moderate Revolution such as he had helped to make in America. He made friends with the Girondins, refused to think ill of Lafayette (now in disgrace), and continued, as an American, to express gratitude to Louis XVI for his share in liberating the United States. By opposing the King's execution down to the last moment, he incurred the hostility of the Jacobins. He was first expelled from the Convention, and then imprisoned as a foreigner; he remained in prison throughout Robespierre's period of power and for some months longer. The responsibility rested only partly with the French; the American Minister, Gouverneur Morris, was equally to blame. He was a Federalist, and sided with England against France; he had, moreover, an ancient personal grudge against Paine for exposing a friend's corrupt deal during the War of Independence. He took the line that Paine was not an American, and that he could therefore do nothing for him. Washington, who was secretly negotiating Jay's treaty with England, was not sorry to have Paine in a situation in which he could not enlighten the French Government as to reactionary opinion in America. Paine escaped the guillotine by accident, but nearly died of illness. At last Morris was replaced by Monroe (of the 'Doctrine'), who immediately procured his release, took him into his own house, and restored him to health by eighteen months' care and kindness.

Paine did not know how great a part Morris had played in his misfortunes, but he never forgave Washington, after whose death, hearing that a statue was to be made of the great man, he addressed the following lines to the sculptor:

> Take from the mine the coldest, hardest stone,
> It needs no fashion: it is Washington.
> But if you chisel, let the stroke be rude,
> And on his heart engrave–Ingratitude.

This remained unpublished, but a long, bitter letter to Washington was published in 1796, ending:

> 'And as to you, Sir, treacherous in private friendship (for so you have been to me, and that in the day of danger) and a hypocrite in public life, the world will be puzzled to decide whether you are an apostate or an impostor; whether you have abandoned good principles, or whether you ever had any.'

To those who know only the statuesque Washington of the legend, these may seem wild words. But 1796 was the year of the first contest for the Presidency, between Jefferson and Adams, in which Washington's whole weight was thrown into support of the latter, in spite of his belief in monarchy and aristocracy; moreover Washington was taking sides with England against France, and doing all in his power to prevent the spread of those republican and democratic principles to which he owed his own elevation. These public grounds, combined with a very grave personal grievance, show that Paine's words were not without justification.

It might have been more difficult for Washington to leave Paine languishing in prison if that rash man had not spent his last days of liberty in giving literary expression to the theological opinions which he and Jefferson shared with Washington and Adams, who, however, were careful to avoid all public avowals of unorthodoxy. Foreseeing his imprisonment, Paine set to work to write *The Age of Reason,* of which he finished Part I six hours before his arrest. This book shocked his contemporaries, even many of those who agreed with his politics. Nowadays, apart from a few passages in bad taste, there is very little that most clergymen would disagree with. In the first chapter he says:

> 'I believe in one God, and no more; and I hope for happiness beyond this life.
> I believe in the equality of man, and I believe that religious duties consist in doing justice, loving mercy, and endeavouring to make our fellow-creatures happy.'

These were not empty words. From the moment of his first participation in public affairs – his protest against slavery in 1775 – down to the day of his death, he was consistently opposed to every form of cruelty, whether practised by his own party or by his opponents. The Government of England at that time was a ruthless oligarchy, using Parliament as a means of lowering the standard of life in the poorest classes; Paine advocated political reform as the only cure for this abomination, and had to fly for his life. In France, for opposing unnecessary bloodshed, he was thrown into prison and narrowly escaped death. In America, for opposing slavery and upholding the principles of the Declaration of Independence, he was abandoned by the Government at the moment when he most needed its support. If, as he maintained and as many now believe, true religion consists in 'doing justice, loving mercy, and endeavouring to make our fellow-creatures happy,' there was not one among his opponents who had as good a claim to be considered a religious man.

The greater part of *The Age of Reason* consists of criticism of the Old Testament from a moral point of view. Very few nowadays would regard the massacres of men, women, and children recorded in the Pentateuch and the Book of Joshua as models of righteousness, but in Paine's day it was considered impious to criticise the Israelites when the Old Testament approved of them. Many pious divines wrote answers to him. The most liberal of those was the Bishop of Llandaff, who went so far as to admit that parts of the Pentateuch were not writtten by Moses, and some of the Psalms were not composed by David. For such concessions he incurred the hostility of George III and lost all chance of translation to a richer see. Some of the Bishop's replies to Paine are curious. For example, *The Age of Reason* ventured to doubt whether God really commanded that all males and married women among the Midianites should be slaughtered, while the maidens should be preserved. The Bishop indignantly retorted that the maidens were not preserved for immoral purposes, as Paine had wickedly suggested, but as slaves, to which there could be no ethical objection. The orthodox of our day have forgotten what orthodoxy was like a hundred and forty years ago. They have forgotten still more completely that it was men like Paine who, in face of persecution, caused the softening of dogma by which our age profits. Even the Quakers refused Paine's request for burial in their cemetery, although a Quaker farmer was one of the very few who followed his body to the grave.

After *The Age of Reason* Paine's work ceased to be important. For a long time he was very ill; when he recovered, he found no scope in the France of the Directoire and the First Consul. Napoleon did not ill-treat him, but naturally had no use for him, except as a possible agent of democratic rebellion in England. He became home-sick for America, remembering his former success and popularity in that country, and wishing to help the Jeffersonians against the Federalists. But the fear of capture by the English, who would have certainly hanged him, kept him in France until the Treaty of Amiens. At length, in October 1802, he landed at Baltimore, and at once wrote to Jefferson (now President):

> 'I arrived here on Saturday from Havre, after a passage of sixty days. I have several cases of models, wheels, etc., and as soon as I can get them from the vessel and put them on board the packet for Georgetown I shall set off to pay my respects to you. Your much obliged fellow-citizen,
>
> Thomas Paine.'

He had no doubt that all his old friends, except such as were Federalists, would welcome him. But there was a difficulty: Jefferson had had a hard fight for the

Presidency, and in the campaign the most effective weapon against him – unscrupulously used by ministers of all denominations – had been the accusation of infidelity. His opponents magnified his intimacy with Paine, and spoke of the pair as 'the two Toms.' Twenty years later, Jefferson was still so much impressed by the bigotry of his compatriots that he replied to a Unitarian minister who wished to publish a letter of his: 'No, my dear Sir, not for the world!...I should as soon undertake to bring the crazy skulls of Bedlam to sound understanding as to inculcate reason into that of an Athanasian...keep me therefore from the fire and faggot of Calvin and his victim Servetus.' It was not surprising that, when the fate of Servetus threatened them, Jefferson and his political followers should have fought shy of too close an association with Paine. He was treated politely, and had no cause to complain, but the old easy friendships were dead.

In other circles he fared worse. Dr. Rush of Philadelphia, one of his first American friends, would have nothing to do with him: 'his principles' he wrote, 'avowed in his *Age of Reason,* were so offensive to me that I did not wish to renew my intercourse with him.' In his own neighbourhood he was mobbed, and refused a seat in the stage coach; in the last year of his life he was not allowed to vote, on the alleged ground of his being a foreigner. He was falsely accused of immorality and intemperance, and his last years were spent in solitude and poverty. He died in 1809. As he was dying, two clergymen invaded his room and tried to convert him, but he merely said 'Let me alone; good morning!' Nevertheless, the orthodox invented a myth of deathbed recantation which was widely believed.

His posthumous fame was greater in England than in America. To publish his works was, of course, illegal, but it was done repeatedly, although many men went to prison for this offence. The last prosecution on this charge was that of Richard Carlile and his wife in 1819: he was sentenced to prison for three years and a fine of £1,500, she to one year and £500. It was in this year that Cobbett brought Paine's bones to England, and established his fame as one of the heroes in the fight for democracy in England. Cobbett did not, however, give his bones a permanent resting place. 'The monument contemplated by Cobbett,' says Moncure Conway,* 'was never raised. There was much parliamentary and municipal excitement. A Bolton town-crier was imprisoned nine weeks for proclaiming the arrival. In 1836 the bones passed with Cobbett's effects into the hands of a receiver (West). The Lord Chancellor refusing to regard them as an asset, they were kept by an old day-labourer until 1844, when they passed to B. Tilley, 13 Bedford Square, London, a furniture dealer...In 1854, Rev. R. Ainslie (Unitarian) told E. Truelove that he owned "the skull and the right hand of Thomas Paine," but evaded subsequent inquiries.' No trace now remains, even of the skull and right hand.

Paine's influence in the world was twofold. During the American Revolution he inspired enthusiasm and confidence, and thereby did much to facilitate victory.

In France his popularity was transient and superficial, but in England he inaugurated the stubborn resistance of plebeian Radicals to the long tyranny of Pitt and Liverpool. His opinions on the Bible, though they shocked his contemporaries more than his unitarianism, were such as might now be held by an Archbishop, but his true followers were the men who worked in the movement that sprang from him – those whom Pitt imprisoned, those who suffered under the Six Acts, the Owenites, Chartists, Trade Unionists, and Socialists. To all these champions of the oppressed he set an example of courage, humanity, and single-mindedness. When public issues were involved he forgot personal prudence. The world decided, as it usually does in such cases, to punish him for his lack of self-seeking; to this day his fame is less than it would have been if his character had been less generous. Some worldly wisdom is required even to secure praise for the lack of it.

*Whose biography of Paine and edition of his works are a monument of patient devotion and careful research.

Tom Paine's bones brought home by Cobbett, and soon lost. His ideas were less easy to mislay.

Skull and Bones

Kurt Vonnegut

I am writing this in July of 2004, so I cannot know whether George W. Bush or John F. Kerry will be our President, God willing, for the next four years. These two Nordic, aristocratic multi-millionaires are virtually twins, and as unlike most of the rest of us as a couple of cross-eyed albinos. But this much I find timely: both candidates were and still are members of the exclusive secret society at Yale, called 'Skull and Bones'. That means that, no matter which one wins, we will have a Skull and Bones President at a time when entire vertebrate species, because of how we have poisoned the topsoil, the waters and the atmosphere, are becoming, *hey presto*, nothing but skulls and bones.

Poetry!

What was the beginning of this end? Some might say Adam and Eve and the apple. I say it was Prometheus, a Titan, a son of gods, who in Greek myth stole fire from his parents and gave it to human beings. The gods were so mad they chained him naked to a rock with his back exposed, and had eagles eat his liver.

And it is now plain that the gods were right to do that. Our close cousins the gorillas and orangs and chimps and gibbon apes have gotten along just fine all this time while eating raw vegetable matter, whereas we not only prepare hot meals, but have now all but destroyed this once salubrious planet as a life-support system in fewer than two hundred years, mainly by making thermodynamic whoopee with fossil fuels.

The Englishman Michael Faraday built the first dynamo only one hundred and seventy-two years ago. The German Karl Benz built the first automobile powered by an internal combustion engine only a hundred and nineteen years ago. The first oil well in the USA, now a dry hole, was drilled in Titusville, Pennsylvania, by Edwin L. Drake only a hundred and forty-five years ago.

The American Wright brothers, of course,

A new book of speeches by Kurt Vonnegut, entitled Man without a Country, *is to be published by 7 Stories Press.*

built and flew the first airplane only a hundred and one years ago. It was powered by gasoline. You want to talk about irresistible whoopee?

A booby trap.

Fossil fuels, so easily set alight! Yes, and as Bush and Kerry are out campaigning, we are probably touching off nearly the very last whiffs and drops and chunks of them. All lights are about to go out. No more electricity. All forms of transportation are about to stop, and the planet Earth will soon have a crust of skulls and bones and dead machinery.

And nobody can do a thing about it. It's too late in the game. Don't spoil the party, but here's the truth: we have squandered our planet's resources, including air and water, as though there were no tomorrow, so now there isn't going to be one.

Empire No More!
by Ken Coates

Wars and threats of war seethe all around us. The end of the Cold War gave place to a frenzied new drive to build more powerful and deadly weapons, and a permanent Orwellian 'war on terror' which is self-renewing, and, it is to be feared, unwinnable. American military doctrine has been transmuted into a formal commitment to 'Full Spectrum Dominance', or unchallengeable superiority in any contest on or in land, sea, air, space or information. The United Nations finds itself widely ignored, and overruled by brute force. The Geneva Conventions are violated wholesale.

Ken Coates was a founder of European Nuclear Disarmament, which tried to take both peace and human rights seriously. Full Spectrum Dominance makes this commitment more difficult, and more necessary, than ever.

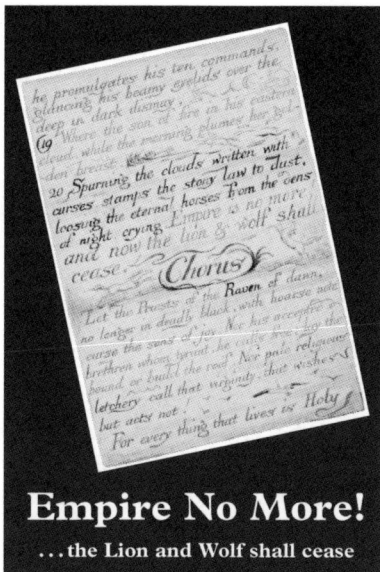

Empire No More!
…the Lion and Wolf shall cease

£11.99 | PB | 0 85124 694 X |
£45 | HB | 0 85124 700 8 | 288pp

No More Hiroshimas
Poems & translations
by James Kirkup

It is almost 60 years since the atomic bombing of Hiroshima and Nagasaki. These events inspired *No More Hiroshimas*, a collection of poems by the distinguished poet James Kirkup, which is belatedly published for the first time in Britain.

> 'These poems all have their roots in one late afternoon at the land workers' hostel outside Ponteland, Northumberland. As we entered the hostel we got the news that the first American Atom Bomb had been dropped on Japan, on the city of Hiroshima. It was the first time we had heard of that place that was to become a universal symbol of man's inhumanity towards his fellow-men.'
> **James Kirkup**

£6.99 | PB | ISBN 0 85124 689 3 | 72pp

www.spokesmanbooks.com
email: elfeuro@compuserve.com
credit/debit cards welcome -
Visa/Mastercard/Switch/Electron/Solo

Available from **Spokesman Books**
(LRB) Russell House, Bulwell Lane,
Nottingham, NG6 0BT, England.
Tel: 0115 9708318 - **Fax:** 0115 9420433

Torture is a Crime

*Inge Genefke
&
Bent Sørensen*

In Spokesman 81, Dr Inge Genefke described how her pioneering work with the victims of torture led her to realise that torture is fundamentally a crime against democracy. Here, she and Professor Bent Sørensen scrutinise the UN Convention against Torture which defines torture and spells out measures for its eradication.

Inge Genefke founded the Danish Rehabilitation and Research Centre for Torture Victims (RCT) in 1982.

Bent Sørensen is the Senior Medical Consultant to the International Rehabilitation Council for Torture Victims (IRCT).

When 'Kolingen', a character created by the Swedish artist Engstroem, passes a shop window containing all kinds of beauty products, he speaks the famous words: 'wonderful that it exists', and, after a short pause, 'a shame that it is necessary'.

Since 1974, medical work against torture has been undertaken in Copenhagen, Denmark. It started with four volunteer doctors, and now extends to nearly 200 rehabilitation centres for torture victims worldwide: 'wonderful that it exists'.

The anti-torture movement provides rehabilitation to the victims of torture, and it strives to put the problem of torture on the agenda, to raise awareness of *where* torture is used, and how *destructive* torture is for every democratisation process. All this work is aimed at breaking the silence which surrounds the problem of torture. The current debate in newspapers and on radio and television has shown that this aim has been achieved: 'A shame that it is necessary'.

Danish politicians, the Chief of Defence, newspapers, editorials and non-governmental organisations all agree: 'torture should not take place'. Many facts have been presented, and many proposals for improvements have been put forward. One aspect seems to be missing, however, and the aim of this article is to emphasise that the necessary international instrument already exists. This instrument takes all problems regarding torture into account – it only needs to be put into effect.

This instrument is the UN Convention against Torture and other Cruel, Inhuman or Degrading Treatment or Punishment. It was adopted – by consensus – by the UN General Assembly on 10 December 1984 (the day which, in 1948, was made UN Human Rights Day), and it came into force on 26 June 1987. (Since 1997, following Denmark's initiative, this day has become the UN International Day in Support of Victims of Torture). The

Convention has been ratified by 134 countries, including all of those that currently have troops in Iraq.

The provisions of the Convention always apply during wartime, when the so-called Geneva Conventions apply, and they always apply during peacetime, when the Geneva Conventions do not apply. This means that the excuse which was used in Afghanistan – 'we are not at war, so the Conventions do no apply, they are not prisoners of war' – is invalid. The Convention against Torture always applies. Contrary to some other conventions, it cannot be suspended, not even partly, and not even temporarily. So, let us use the Convention as our legal framework – if it is good enough! We will now take a look to see if it is.

Article 1 defines torture – not 'other cruel, inhuman or degrading treatment or punishment'. These concepts are not defined and probably never will be. Four conditions must apply in order to fulfil the definition of torture. If one of these conditions is missing, it is not torture.

The act must:
1) cause 'severe pain or suffering, whether physical or mental'
2) be 'intentionally inflicted'

We think that most people know – or can easily imagine – that torture makes you ill. Torture is the only illness that is 'intentional' – all other illnesses are caused by bacteria, viruses, cancer, and so on. Torture is inflicted by another human being, and this absurdity makes the after-effects even more unbearable.

Further:
3) The act of torture must be perpetrated for a purpose. The Convention mentions many possible purposes. The most well known, presumably, is the wish to get information or to obtain a confession, but the Convention also mentions intimidation or coercion of the victim or a third person (please remember the pictures from Iraq!).

Torture is a very bad way of obtaining confessions or information: after some time, the victim will always say whatever the perpetrator wants to hear, and will be willing to sign blank pieces of paper. When we teach, we usually say to the police: 'Do you want the truth, or do you want a confession?'

Finally:
4) The torture must be inflicted by or with the consent or acquiescence of a public official.

This just makes matters worse: the state is behind the torture.

Article 2 prohibits the use of torture with complete clarity: 'No exceptional circumstances whatsoever, whether a state of war or a threat of war, internal political instability or any other public emergency, may be invoked as a justification of torture.' This means *no torture*. It means *no torture* of terrorists. It means torture can *never* be justified with reference to a 'ticking bomb', *not even* if we use the justification that 'we can save 200 lives if we torture one man'. Torture as defined in article 1 should never take place.

Section 3 of Article 2 states: 'An order from a superior officer or a public authority may not be invoked as a justification of torture.' This must be one of the most far-reaching provisions, and it also applies to the armed forces. The basic premiss within the armed forces is that you obey an order, otherwise it is mutiny. If the order (or the content of a written instruction) is to 'use all means', then the answer is: 'no, not torture'. 'If I, (the subordinate) use torture, I am guilty of a criminal offence and should be punished. And the person who gave the order is also a criminal and should be punished.' Article 2 therefore offers protection against every kind of torture at the same time as it offers legal protection to those people who refuse to torture others.

No less than 5 Articles (nos. 4 to 8) deal with the punishment of perpetrators. In summary, it is the obligation of the state to ensure:
– that torture, as defined in article 1, is an offence under the criminal law of the country
– that persons who are accused of torture are taken to court and, if found guilty, are given penalties which take into account the 'grave nature' of the offences.

Furthermore, there is no period of limitation for the crime of torture, and it is not possible to grant amnesty for the crime of torture. So, if President Bush, shortly before the November elections, wishes to pardon soldiers who have committed crimes during the fighting in Iraq, he will have to exclude the perpetrators of torture. In the rehabilitation centres we often say that *perhaps* the victims can forgive the perpetrators, society cannot do so on their behalf.

Torture is an international crime to a greater degree than crimes against humanity or genocide. An example illustrates this: a Danish citizen has, on an order from the United States Department of Defence, tortured a Jordanian citizen while he was in Afghanistan. Later, the Dane is on holiday in the United Kingdom. It will then be the obligation (not just a possibility or a right) of the United Kingdom to take the Dane into custody, or to take other legal measures to ensure his presence while investigations are made. The prosecutor is then obliged to deal with the case as he or she does with all other cases of a serious nature, and if the inquiry leads to proceedings being brought, then the case should proceed in a British court, unless the Dane is extradited to a country where legal proceedings would be instituted.

With respect to the crime of torture, the Convention against Torture makes the International Criminal Court (of which the United States is not a member) superfluous.

The rules of the Convention against Torture apply to everyone, including Heads of State and former Heads of State. Only the question of diplomatic immunity has not yet been solved. The Danish Ministry of Justice has declined to express its view in this matter, but referred it to the Ministry of Foreign

Affairs, where they were of the opinion that diplomatic immunity also applies in cases of the international crime of torture. This contradicts the view of the UN Committee against Torture.

Five of the articles in the Convention aim to counteract impunity. Alleged perpetrators are to be brought before a court, irrespective of the nationality of the perpetrator or the victim, or of the place where the crime took place. If the perpetrator is found guilty, he must receive a penalty which takes into account the grave nature of the crime.

In addition to the perpetrator, there is also a victim, perhaps several. This is dealt with in Article 14. The state is obliged to offer the victim of torture a 'fair and adequate compensation, including the means for as full rehabilitation as possible', and this means medical rehabilitation. It is the state that has the duty to offer this. The victim must not be required to press charges against the perpetrators or the state. Recently, initiatives have been taken to offer medical rehabilitation to the victims of torture in Iraq.

What about prevention?

Article 10 deals with education, and the Convention states: 'Each State Party shall ensure that education and information regarding the prohibition against torture are fully included in the training of law enforcement personnel, civil or military, medical personnel, public officials and other persons who may be involved in the custody, interrogation or treatment of any individual subjected to any form of arrest, detention or imprisonment.'

The message is quite clear: all personnel, civil as well as military, who serve in the armed forces or in peace-keeping forces must be trained in the prohibition of torture and in the ways in which this prohibition is secured in practice. It is not enough for them to be taught about human rights in general or about the Geneva Conventions. US Army Major General Antonio Taguba's criticism and his request for education were therefore completely justified – it is a plain obligation to educate these personnel groups.

The Major General also asked for control and supervision. Article 11 deals with this: 'Each State Party shall keep under systematic review interrogation rules, instructions, methods and practices as well as arrangements for the custody and treatment of persons subjected to any form of arrest, detention or imprisonment in any territory under its jurisdiction, with a view to preventing any cases of torture.'

If the United States had complied with Article 11, as the country has committed to, these problems would not have occurred. Article 11 and Articles 1-8 provide the legal framework for dealing with the problems we are now facing.

Who is going to investigate?

Article 12 says: 'Each State Party shall ensure that its competent authorities proceed to a prompt and impartial investigation (…) of any act of torture', and Article 13: 'any individual (…) has been subjected to torture (…) has the right to complain to, and to have his case promptly and impartially examined by, its competent authorities.' There is therefore no doubt that the legal basis exists in the United States for an inquiry into what has taken place in prisons.

Finally, Article 15 states: '(…) any statement which (…) has been made as a result of torture shall not be invoked as evidence in any proceedings.' So, military and police personnel should know that they waste their time if they get a confession through torture – the confession is useless.

Relevant personnel therefore have to learn and understand that torture is prohibited always, including when an order is given to torture. In addition to being illegal and punishable, torture is also degrading for the victim, the perpetrator and society as a whole. Finally, if a confession is the objective, using torture renders it worthless.

In discussions such as these, the question of the validity of information obtained by the use of torture is frequently asked: how does this information compare to the information obtained by normal means? Only a few studies have been carried out. In Peru, it has been shown that the police could trust the information that people had given during ordinary interrogations, whereas those who had been tortured simply admitted anything, making the information useless. This means that – in addition to all the above-mentioned aspects – torture is also a very ineffective working practice.

What if the United States does not comply with the Convention?

Perhaps Article 20 can be used: 'If the Committee [the UN Committee against Torture] receives reliable information which appears to it to contain well-founded indications that torture is being systematically practised (…) the Committee shall invite the State Party to co-operate in the examination of the information.' This may lead to a visit to the respective country (a so-called Article 20-visit).

The Committee has 10 members. As a member of the Committee from its inception in 1988 until 2000, one of the authors (Bent Sørensen) has gained a substantial amount of knowledge about the work of the Committee and its members. They are all literate, for a start, and therefore they have received reliable information on the United States and Iraq from, among others, Donald Rumsfeld (if he says it is torture, it probably is). The pictures represent what the Convention calls 'well-founded indications'. 'Torture is being systematically practised' – yes, it takes place in specific prisons and under specific circumstances, so it must be said to be systematic. In this light, we are of the opinion that the Committee could undertake an Article 20-investigation and inspect the conditions.

In conclusion, the Convention against Torture contains all the necessary provisions to be able to punish perpetrators, to compensate, prevent, control, educate and inspect: it is adequate.

European Social Forum London

14-17 October 2004

RMT welcomes the European Social Forum

No to privatisation

Globalisation for people, not for profit

Bob Crow
General Secretary

Tony Donaghey
President

Another World Is Possible

The European Social Forum Comes to London

Ken Coates

Ken Coates' new book, Empire No More! *is just published by Spokesman (£11.99).*

The European Social Forum was inspired by the World Social Forum in Porto Alegre. This defined itself in distinction from the World Economic Forum at Davos, which took on its shoulders all the sins of neo-liberalism with the globalisation of greed. An impressive list of participants has been assembled from non-governmental organisations in a wide variety of countries. Now the European Social Forum will come to London, at the invitation of a number of activist groupings, with the support of London Mayor, Ken Livingstone. We are bound to wish it well, because there is a great vacuum where consequent political discussion used to take place, and there are many urgent social issues about which informed people need to share their experiences. It remains to be seen how widely the Social Forum will be able to cast its net, when it comes to England.

In several European countries at the same time, there are a number of key problems which would clearly benefit from joint analysis, and if it could be achieved, common action.

It is not difficult to see why the European Social Forums have established a prototype for this kind of convergence. Basing themselves on the traditions, and the Charter of Principles agreed by the World Social Forum (see p.38), which met in Porto Alegre, Brazil, the European Social Forum met first of all in Florence, and then, last year, in Paris. Each gathering attracted tens of thousands of participants, from a very wide variety of social movements, non-governmental organisations and trade unions.

The slogan of the World Social Forum, 'Another World is Possible', touched a vein of idealism and commitment which fired many young people to identify with it. It stood out in clear contrast to the compromised behaviour of so many established institutions in Europe, including, unhappy to say, many governments and established political parties. The World Social Forum made clear its opposition to 'the process of globalisation commanded by the large multinational corporations and by the governments and international institutions (which are) at the service of these corporations' interests'. It was able to draw on the practical experiences of non-governmental organisations and aid organisations, as well as movements in defence of the environment and community organisations with a wide variety of aims.

The World Social Forum found itself confronting a global power structure: but it did not retreat into parochialism, seeking instead to find the way to an alternative world. Just as it was finding new bases for coherence, the rising tide of militarism engulfed the world in new conflicts, culminating in the dreadful invasion of Iraq, in which Iraqi sources have identified thirty-seven thousand civilian deaths. (The Blitz of the Luftwaffe in England killed twenty-two thousand people.)

So it was that this continuing international discussion reached out from engaging with myriad social problems to embracing the growing world-wide peace movement. A predominant element of spontaneity governed this process, which represented a coming together of many tributaries, innumerable initiatives, and centres of goodwill.

In Britain, a political crisis which had already shown itself in numerous other European countries was becoming evident and acute. For decades, dissent in all its forms, and pressures of innumerable reforms, had found their focus in the Labour Party. Of course, not every critic of the established society could join that Party, but all were likely to find their behaviour influenced by it. But openness to all the schools of rebellion became identified with sterile oppositionism, and a new generation of political leaders arose which sought out and established a new conformity, based upon manipulation and media consent, and ruthless accommodation to the established powers. Assiduous courtship of the Murdoch news empire was but a token of the engagement of this new political establishment. No wonder it became important for any idealist, and all those alien to cynicism, to insist that 'another world is possible'. Legions of non-governmental activists, trade union members, Church militants and other volunteers found the prevailing official climate of public organisations increasingly oppressive. Even when good actions were performed by government, they were usually overlaid with spin and wider deception.

That is why, in England, there is a great deal of space for the European Social Forum, if it can maintain its ready traditions of openness and engagement with the important issues which continue to trouble our society.

One of these is clearly mass unemployment. In England, followers of the official statistics believe that this problem has been solved. But scholars who are willing to dig deeper, think not. Christina Beatty and Stephen Fothergill have looked in depth at the numbers of long-term sickness claimants, many of whom, for a considerable time, have been refugees from the provision for unemployment relief. They have concluded that, in parts of England, in the north, as well as in Scotland and Wales, there are some two and a half million unemployed people, who depend on sickness related benefits to keep body and soul together, although in fact there are no jobs for them. The employment position in England has eased in recent years, but this level of hardship remains quite unacceptable.

When I was in the European Parliament, I drew on the earlier calculations of Stephen Fothergill and his colleagues in the course of preparing two pan-European Conventions of unemployed people, which met in the Parliament building in Brussels, and enabled the unemployed and sympathetic scholars and activists to compare notes and co-ordinate their efforts for the recovery of jobs. These Conventions drew support from all the main political Groups in the European Parliament, although they were initiated by members of the Socialist, Green and United Left Groups. Three of the most energetic activists in the European Parliament, who supported these initiatives, are no longer Members. But there are very many reasons why a forum of the unemployed is necessary, and indeed has become more necessary than it was, as the problem of unemployment has worsened in a number of countries, and gone underground in others.

These initiatives were part of a broader attempt to bring together groupings within civil society, in order to reinforce political attempts to deal with problems. My first initiative in this respect was the Pensioners' Parliament, which the European Parliament's Socialist Group agreed to promote, and which brought together five hundred-plus pensioners from every country in the European Union, to seek to compare provision and experiences between one country and another, and to try to agree on common goals. This meeting was deemed to have been very successful, so much so that it was repeated the following year as a joint initiative of all the Groups in the European Parliament.

I was very pleased when, quite spontaneously, a group of disabled people came to the European Parliament to ask for hospitality for a parliament of European disabled people. At first, many of the Parliament's officials were very sceptical about this request, but a powerful lobby among the handicapped, the blind, the deaf, and the victims of a wide range of disabilities, after a lobby of the wheelchairs and white sticks, won the agreement of a majority of Members of the Parliament, and the Disabled People's Parliament duly met in the newly opened hemicycle in Brussels. I was asked to give a brief opening speech, where I learnt the meaning of a prolonged session of waving by members of the audience. This, I was informed, was deaf people's applause.

The idea of the Social Forums is wider, and potentially more creative, since it can bring together people from an immense diversity of organisations, NGOs and specialist groups, and help to empower them by enriching the field of their contacts.

Previous efforts to develop wider associations of NGOs in practical collaboration tended to find their focus in the existing political organisations. But today it is a mark of gathering social crisis that worse problems are accompanied by fewer official openings for redress. Old social democracies sought to manage change in society. Now, with some skill, they seek to understand and to manage change in the reporting of society, and the systematic manipulation and under-weighting of its bad news. Thus we get a flow of tainted information, misleading statistics, fabricated intelligence. Today we have the age of the official lie. That is why inclusive and comprehensive meetings are so valuable, and should certainly be continued and developed.

But the experience of our people insists that another world is really possible, and invites us to move beyond our general forum, towards more specific and conventional meetings of minds, tracing out the lineaments of that other practice which will bring the other world into fruition.

Bakers, Food & Allied Workers Union

*Suuporting workers in struggle
Wherever they may be.*

Joe Marino   General Secretary
Ronnie Draper   President
Jackie Mander   Vice President

Stanborough House,
Great North Road,
Stanborough,
Welwyn Garden City,
Hertfordshire. AL8 7TA
Phone 01707 260150& 01707 259450
www.bfawu.org

Charter of Principles

World Social Forum

Approved and adopted in São Paulo, on April 9, 2001, by the organizations that make up the World Social Forum Organizing Committee; approved with modifications by the World Social Forum International Council on June 10, 2001.

The committee of Brazilian organizations that conceived of, and organized, the first World Social Forum, held in Porto Alegre from January 25th to 30th, 2001, after evaluating the results of that Forum and the expectations it raised, consider it necessary and legitimate to draw up a Charter of Principles to guide the continued pursuit of that initiative. While the principles contained in this Charter – to be respected by all those who wish to take part in the process and to organize new editions of the World Social Forum – are a consolidation of the decisions that presided over the holding of the Porto Alegre Forum and ensured its success, they extend the reach of those decisions and define orientations that flow from their logic.

1. The World Social Forum is an open meeting place for reflective thinking, democratic debate of ideas, formulation of proposals, free exchange of experiences and interlinking for effective action, by groups and movements of civil society that are opposed to neoliberalism and to domination of the world by capital and any form of imperialism, and are committed to building a planetary society directed towards fruitful relationships among Humankind and between it and the Earth.

2. The World Social Forum at Porto Alegre was an event localized in time and place. From now on, in the certainty proclaimed at Porto Alegre that 'another world is possible', it becomes a permanent process of seeking and building alternatives, which cannot be reduced to the events supporting it.

3. The World Social Forum is a world process. All the meetings that are held as part of this process have an international dimension.

4. The alternatives proposed at the World Social Forum stand in opposition to a process of globalization commanded by the large multinational corporations and by the governments and international institutions at the service of those corporations' interests, with the complicity of national governments. They are designed to ensure that globalization in solidarity will prevail as a new stage in world history. This will respect universal human rights, and those of all citizens – men and women – of all nations and the environment and will rest on democratic international systems and institutions at the service of social justice, equality and the sovereignty of peoples.

5. The World Social Forum brings together and interlinks only organizations and movements of civil society from all the countries in the world, but intends neither to be a body representing world civil society.

6. The meetings of the World Social Forum do not deliberate on behalf of the World Social Forum as a body. No-one, therefore, will be authorized, on behalf of any of the editions of the Forum, to express positions claiming to be those of all its participants. The participants in the Forum shall not be called on to take decisions as a body, whether by vote or acclamation, on declarations or proposals for action that would commit all, or the majority, of them and that propose to be taken as establishing positions of the Forum as a body. It thus does not constitute a locus of power to be disputed by the participants in its meetings, nor does it intend to constitute the only option for interrelation and action by the organizations and movements that participate in it.

7. Nonetheless, organizations or groups of organizations that participate in the Forum's meetings must be assured the right, during such meetings, to deliberate on declarations or actions they may decide on, whether singly or in coordination with other participants. The World Social Forum undertakes to circulate such decisions widely by the means at its disposal, without directing, hierarchizing, censuring or restricting them, but as deliberations of the organizations or groups of organizations that made the decisions.

8. The World Social Forum is a plural, diversified, non-confessional, non-governmental and non-party context that, in a decentralized fashion, interrelates organizations and movements engaged in concrete action at levels from the local to the international to build another world.

9. The World Social Forum will always be a forum open to pluralism and to the diversity of activities and ways of engaging of the organizations and movements that decide to participate in it, as well as the diversity of genders, ethnicities, cultures, generations and physical capacities, providing they abide by this Charter of Principles. Neither party representations nor military organizations shall participate in the Forum. Government leaders and members of legislatures who accept the commitments of this Charter may be invited to participate in a personal capacity.

10. The World Social Forum is opposed to all totalitarian and reductionist views of economy, development and history and to the use of violence as a means of social control by the State. It upholds respect for Human Rights, the practices of real democracy, participatory democracy, peaceful relations, in equality and solidarity, among people, ethnicities, genders and peoples, and condemns all forms of domination and all subjection of one person by another.

11. As a forum for debate, the World Social Forum is a movement of ideas that prompts reflection, and the transparent circulation of the results of that reflection, on the mechanisms and instruments of domination by capital, on means and actions to resist and overcome that domination, and on the alternatives proposed to solve the problems of exclusion and social inequality that the process of capitalist globalization with its racist, sexist and environmentally destructive dimensions is creating internationally and within countries.

12. As a framework for the exchange of experiences, the World Social Forum encourages understanding and mutual recognition among its participant organizations and movements, and places special value on the exchange among them, particularly on all that society is building to centre economic activity and political action on meeting the needs of people and respecting nature, in the present and for future generations.

13. As a context for interrelations, the World Social Forum seeks to strengthen and create new national and international links among organizations and movements of society, that – in both public and private life – will increase the capacity for non-violent social resistance to the process of dehumanization the world is undergoing and to the violence used by the State, and reinforce the humanizing measures being taken by the action of these movements and organizations.

14. The World Social Forum is a process that encourages its participant organizations and movements to situate their actions, from the local level to the national level and seeking active participation in international contexts, as issues of planetary citizenship, and to introduce onto the global agenda the change-inducing practices that they are experimenting in building a new world in solidarity.

The Europe We Need

Robin Blackburn

Europe today faces three shocks which threaten its social institutions and aspiration for an independent role in world affairs. They are the shock of rampant United States power, the shock of Anglo-Saxon economics, and the shock of a poorly planned European Union enlargement. While these processes have a long-term character, they now possess enough concentrated force to paralyse European institutions, and to subject the continent to corporate-led globalisation domestically and to United States 'leadership', as the White House now calls its imperial role in global affairs. This is not the Europe the world – or its own citizens – needs.

Because the European Union is, at present, the only global entity with an economic weight and political potential equal to that of the United States, it has – in principle – the best possibility of defying the new hegemon. This should not at all be a question of making Europe more like the United States – a process which has already gone too far – but, instead, of ensuring that Europe represents a different social model and that on the international stage it refuses to chain itself to the chariot wheels of the Bush regime.

Europe's leaders trail behind the United States

Europe has an opportunity for a creative response to the challenges it faces. This is partly because US leadership is itself in deep difficulties, above all in Iraq and the Middle East. And it is also because the sterile formula of Europe's own grotesquely-named 'growth and stability' pact has been breached by the European Union's two leading core states. This represents a break with the baneful rule of the European Central Bank and its disastrous monetarist dogmas.

Europe's response to the impasse of US strategy in Iraq, and to the crisis of European Union monetary governance, does not measure up to the opportunity presented. Rather, it

---

Robin Blackburn is an editor of New Left Review and the author of Banking on Death, or Investing in Life: the History and Future of Pensions, *published by Verso. He teaches in the Sociology Department at the University of Essex and can be reached on roblack@essex.ac.uk*

weakens Europe and betrays the hopes of peoples around the world who would like to see some check on US power.

The Nato allies protest publicly or privately about US 'unilateralism', but then proceed to endorse its consequences. The main Nato powers voted in the United Nations to give the US occupation and its plans a quite unwarranted post-facto legitimacy. As the United States gets into deeper trouble it will again expect its meeker allies to send more troops; that is to put their own citizens in harm's way, in order temporarily to contain a dangerous situation. George W. Bush and Colin Powell are already pursuing this policy, but John Kerry claims that he would have greater success.

At home, the rule of the European Central Bank will be rescued and recycled by giving even greater scope to explicit and 'implicit' privatisation. The latter is the process whereby public services and social protections are degraded in order to oblige the mass of citizens to buy social protection from rapacious finance and insurance houses. Blair, Rafarin, Schröder and Berlusconi have all been pursuing such commodification of social insurance and educational provision. Each have curbed pension provision, and created new opportunities for the financial services industry. However, the latter are looking for more generous tax relief for those who buy their products, a tax subsidy that would absorb much of their costly marketing. The next charge of the 'reformers' will be led by Nicholas Sarkozy, the French finance minister, and José Manuel Barroso, the newly appointed president of the European Commission.

The new course has encountered large-scale, but episodic, resistance: the peace demonstrations of 15 February 2003, strikes and demonstrations against pension cutbacks, opposition to student fees, the rejection of the government in the French local elections, the defeat of Aznar in Spain, and the drubbing administered to New Labour and most other ruling parties in the European elections in June 2004. Continuing attacks on education and welfare will create excellent opportunities to challenge the misleaders of Europe, and to open up conflicts and fissures in the 'grand coalition' of Schröder and Raffarin, Chirac and Sarkozy, Berlusconi and Blair. The disarray of the ruling parties furnishes an opportunity to spell out the core elements of an alternative to neo-liberal Europe.

But whether at home or abroad this alternative must break openly and clearly with what has gone before. In Spain, Zapatero, the Socialist leader, won because he had strongly opposed Spanish backing for the US invasion and occupation of Iraq. Europe's leaders have yet to register the political defeat that the occupiers have already suffered. There is only one way that a future Iraqi government could acquire legitimacy and that is to insist on the complete evacuation of occupation troops, the return of Iraqi oil and the cancellation of the decrees and acts of the occupation authority. If Europe backed the evacuation of the occupying forces, this would not only offer the chance for a new start in Iraq but would chime in with the hopes of tens of millions of Americans.

Europe's leaders also refuse to face the reality that the US economic model, far from being worthy of emulation, is today mired in failure. The collapse of

Enron was just the beginning of a rash of scandals which involve every leading financial institution on Wall Street. Over the last two years, Eliot Spitzer, the New York attorney general, has brought forward investigations and charges which show the large US banks and 'mutual funds' to have been allowing hedge funds to 'skim' (rob) the pension accounts of over ninety million savers. This was the consequence of de-regulation and 'financialisation'. It is accompanied by extravagant returns to chief executives and financial intermediaries, and heavy erosion of pension fund assets.

As 'Anglo-Saxon' economics advance in Europe, it has similar effects – without, so far, an Eliot Spitzer to expose their full scope. Europe now has its own string of corporate scandals – Parmalat, Shell, Vivendi, Ahold and others. These testify to the corroding effect of financial engineering and show how the latest ingenious products of the international banks and accounting firms can give new scope to age-old European traditions of élite corruption. Pension funds have been hit and many have seen their savings shrink. While new scope is given to the commercial banks and insurance houses, social gains such as the 35 hour week are being driven back by employers who can threaten re-location. Meanwhile, as the *Wall Street Journal* headline puts it, 'European CEO Pay is Taking Off'.[1]

Anglo-American corporate welfare destroys good jobs

The US recession of 2000-3 destroyed two and a half million 'good' jobs, and the current weak recovery has seen few of those jobs replaced. The US public rightly worries that the regime of commercial social insurance, which excludes a fifth or more of the population, will fail even most of those it does cover over the next decade or two. Private pensions and health care suffer from a severe 'cost disease'. Competitive marketing consumes vast amounts of money while 'customising' provision for each individual is costly and cumbersome. The loss of manufacturing jobs is also rooted in the problems of large manufacturing concerns which now have large pension fund deficits (in the US these now total $350 billion, in the UK £65 billion).

Many on the US left look to Europe for an alternative, but are increasingly disappointed when they do so. It is true that social protection remains far better in Europe. But even governments of the Left – like that of the Social Democrats and Greens in Germany – lacking the courage and imagination to find better ways to finance welfare, cut benefits instead. This is what Prodi's centre-left government in Italy did in the late 1990s and what he will do again if he ousts Berlusconi.

It is understandable that governments of the Left decline further to raise the already heavy taxes on employment. These taxes are generally not 'progressive'. They fall heavily on workers earning only average or low salaries. Laying a 'tax wedge' of 40 per cent on average incomes, they consequently weaken demand and discourage high rates of employment. With officially-recognised unemployment running at 10 per cent, and many of the unemployed not even getting on the register, certain categories of the population – above all the under-25s and the over-50s – have been condemned to poverty and idleness. Not surprisingly, the demagogues of the far right have often flourished in these conditions.

If we compare the Anglo-Saxon economies with Europe we find that they generate different types of unemployment. Europe's high 'payroll taxes' weaken demand and deter the creation of formal jobs in the service sector, helping to explain why employment rates amongst the proportion of the population aged 18-65 are ten to fifteen percentage points lower than in the United States or the United Kingdom.[2]

But the 'Anglo-Saxon' tradition of encouraging corporations to furnish tax-subsidised pension and health benefits has had a devastating impact on manufacturing employment. Many famous Anglo-American corporations find it impossible to maintain healthy levels of investment and employment because they are weighed down by pension and health deficits. Companies such as Ford, Boeing, American Airlines, US Steel, Goodyear, Maytag, Colgate-Palmolive, Unilever, BT, Rolls Royce and GKN have deficits in their pension funds worth more than half the value of the corporation itself. They are forced to divert huge sums of money to remedy those deficits and to fire thousands of employees.

The Anglo-American corporate welfare schemes are 'pro-cyclical'. That is to say that, during good times, the employers can take a 'contribution holiday' because the value of the shares in the fund rises. British corporations skipped £28 billion of pension fund contributions between 1988 and 2000, which is part of the reason that they are in deep deficit today. In bad times, when it is most difficult, the sponsoring corporation has to stump up cash, because the value of shares in the fund has dropped. The better designed European corporate schemes at least require companies to put away more as special 'reserves' in good times, when it is easier to do so. But all types of corporate-sponsored welfare have the drawback that they are linked to one company, which may itself fail, leaving employees with depleted benefits. In July, the collapse of Federal Mogul, a car parts supplier, halved the pension benefit of 20,000 British workers and cut the expected benefit of a further 20,000 in an associated company.

The pension fund promises that companies make are legally enforceable. This means they take precedence over current investment and current employees. The structure of corporate welfare encourages, or even obliges, companies in difficulties to rob Peter to pay Paul – or rather to sack Peter to pay Paul. The need to bale out pension funds has destroyed hundreds of thousands of jobs in high-end manufacturing in the United States. Likewise in the United Kingdom, manufacturing has been losing 5,000 jobs a week, but Gordon Brown, the Labour Chancellor, has maintained the overall employment level by creating more than half a million jobs in the public sector. (Also note that the real extent of UK unemployment is concealed by the fact that 2.3 million receive 'incapacity benefit', a figure four times as great as 20 years ago.) The end result is that, despite all the weakness of the continental European economy, its exports and manufacturing corporations are stronger than those of the United Kingdom and the United States.

It should be clear that Europe needs a better way of paying for proper old age and health protection than it has – but also a better one than the Anglo-American paths of individualisation or corporate welfare. We need to find other ways to finance the social programmes we need. There are still many positive features of the European social model. Working hours are short, but productivity is high. Decent health care is more widely available than in the United Kingdom, let alone the United States, with its inflated commercial charges. Europe's often beautiful countryside, its many handsome towns and cities, and the successful rehabilitation of several formerly-blighted industrial zones, all testify that a sense of the integrity of public space has not yet been entirely lost.

But the best way to defend what is good in the European social model is to go on the offensive, elaborating a new political economy, one capable of finding needed resources to underwrite social programmes, and of reigning in, and ultimately controlling, the forces of financialisation.

The share levy: a new way to finance future social spending

It is now some time since governments of the Left dared to ask whether the owners of the large corporations might be obliged to contribute more to the wider society, without which their own profits would be impossible. The most far-seeing attempt to think through the types of new finance that would be needed to guarantee generous social provision was Rudolf Meidner's advocacy of 'wage-earner funds' in the 1970s and 1980s.

Rudolf Meidner was – together with Gosta Rehn – the architect of the Swedish welfare state. He was Chief Economist of the LO, Sweden's main trade union federation. He produced an impressive body of policy-oriented economic analysis that deserved – and still deserves – to win the Nobel Prize. A distinguishing feature of his approach was that the working of social funds was harmonised with both a wage-bargaining round and the protection of high employment levels.

Anticipating the new social expenditures that would be entailed by an ageing and learning society he argued for the setting up of strategic social funds to be financed by a share levy. This did not work like traditional corporate taxation, which subtracts from cash-flow and, potentially, investment. Instead Meidner's levy falls on wealthy shareholders, the value of whose holdings is diluted, not on the resources of the corporation as a productive concern. According to the original plan every company with more than fifty employees was obliged to issue new shares every year equivalent to 20 per cent of its profits. The newly issued shares – which could not be sold for several years – were to be given to a network of 'wage earner funds', representing trade unions and local authorities. The latter would hold the shares, and reinvest the income they yielded from dividends, in order to finance future social expenditure. As the wage earner funds grew they would be able to play an increasing part in directing policy in the corporations which they owned.[3]

Meidner's visionary scheme was strongly supported by trade unions and the members of the Social Democratic party, but strongly opposed by the privately owned media, and by the 'twenty families' who dominate the country's large corporations. After a scare campaign the Social Democratic government eventually withdrew the proposed share levy but set up social funds financed by a profits tax. These were wound up by the incoming Conservatives in 1992. So Meidner's plan has yet to be tried.

The need for a new layer of European social provision

The visible crumbling of Europe's ability to protect its own citizens weakens its voice in world affairs. A determined effort to rescue its collapsing social model could be achieved if the Union itself sponsored at least some new social provision for all citizens. Interestingly enough, this was the approach of President Franklin Roosevelt in the 1930s when the United States faced its own most serious social crisis. The Social Security Act of 1935 became the so-called 'third rail' of US politics. Eventually it covered everyone and the Social Security card became a badge of civic identity.

US Social Security redistributed from rich to poor – including from rich regions to poor ones – in ways that promoted a minimum of national unity. The European Union today has no social programmes. The best it has are so-called 'convergence' funds, the Common Agricultural Policy and schemes targeted at new members. But these do not cover everybody, as does Social Security, and have much less resources than the US programme. While the Common Agricultural Policy has a budget of 50 billion euros each year – roughly $45 billion – US Social Security has a budget of nearly $400 billion annually to pay old age and disability pensions for forty million US citizens.

Of course, US Social Security is far less generous than most European equivalents, and is today threatened with privatisation by President Bush. Nevertheless it does help to bind together the citizens of the different states and to help focus loyalty to the political order.

Three economists – James Galbraith, Pedro Conceicao and Pedro Ferreira – have argued for a 'truly European welfare state, with a continental retirement programme' and 'the creation of major new universities of the first water…in the beautiful, lower income regions of the European periphery and the full funding of students to attend them.'[4]

A Europe-wide welfare regime could also encourage better child-care provision. The problem of the ageing society is as much the result of a low birth rate as it is of increased longevity. It is striking that today Scandinavia, with its generous attention to child care, has a much higher birth rate than Mediterranean Europe. It is also interesting that the introduction of the 35 hour week in France coincided with a small but significant recovery in the French birth rate. Improvements to social welfare, education and working conditions should be pursued for their own sake, but they will often contribute to a broader social framework of well-being.

A European-wide welfare regime should be organised on a universal basis so that every citizen and every country receives some benefit. Special supplements might be available on a regional basis so that poorer regions in the wealthier states would also benefit.

If a European Union-wide Meidner-style corporate levy – set initially at ten per cent of corporate profits – was introduced, the resources raised could be put in the hands of regional networks of democratically-administered social funds. This should be conceived of as an addition to – not a replacement of – national welfare policies which, where necessary, might also be able to draw on emergency help from the Europe-wide fund. Levied on a continent-wide basis, the arrangements would contribute towards 'tax harmonisation' and help to deter social dumping. The new member states have low corporate taxes – Estonia's are to be zero on reinvested profits – while their income taxes are broadly similar to those in many parts of Western Europe. Under a share levy scheme wherever corporations were located they would have to issue new shares to the social funds based on their profits anywhere in Europe. Two-thirds of the yield would be distributed to the fund network inside each member country and one-third would be distributed on a continent-wide basis in proportion to population. So the social funds located in new member states would benefit from a central as well as local distribution. This would not only help them to raise expenditure on social and educational purposes but also give their local funds greater leverage, as institutional shareholders, over the multinational corporations.

It might be objected that if the powerful Swedish Social Democrats and trade unions were defeated when they tried to introduce such a measure, why is there any reason to think that something similar could be achieved in the new Europe where labour is now much weaker? My answer would be that there are four reasons why the outcome could be different. Firstly, European corporations are not as tightly organised and cohesive as Sweden's twenty families. Secondly, recent social mobilisations in Europe have been stronger and more persistent on pensions than any other issue. Thirdly, ruling parties have proved to be exceptionally vulnerable when they try to weaken and undermine social provision. Fourthly, it would be possible to frame the social fund proposals in ways that anticipate the sort of opposition that blocked advance in Sweden.

The share levy at ten per cent of profits would have the effect of diluting the value of all shares by about one per cent. Contrary to myth, individual shareholding is still confined to a small minority in Europe. Nevertheless bona fide pension funds also hold shares and it might be claimed that they would lose out. Most would be likely to gain more than they lost by the levy – if there was any doubt about this, they could be directly compensated by an allocation from the social funds.

The ownership of shares is still very unequal so the levy would work like a wealth tax. Unlike other attempts to tax wealth the share levy would not fall on home ownership or small farms and businesses – to meet this problem wealth taxes invariably allow exemptions which turn into handy loop-holes and reduce the value of the revenue they raise. Other revenue sources which could be tapped to boost social and educational expenditure would be a tax on increases in the value of commercial land and a tax on fossil fuels. Together these levies and taxes would ensure that corporations would help to finance the social fabric on which their operations entirely depend and to give all citizens a share in the fruits of economic advance.

The European Trade Union Confederation has long called for the setting up of a proper, continent-wide Social Fund, with resources which it could invest to generate productive employment and that could underwrite future welfare expenditure. In 1959, the then European Community established a European Investment Bank, which was meant to counter-balance the power of the central banks. With the scrapping of the 'growth and stability pact' there is more than ever a role for the European Investment Bank. Indeed, three Cambridge economists have argued that the European Investment Bank should be built up as a counter-weight to the European Central Bank.[5]

The social funds would also be as much about producing wealth as distributing it. In a continent where stock exchanges are already of greatly increased importance, the social funds could help to protect productive enterprises from 'financialisation', to promote socially responsible business objectives, and to assert a degree of popular control over the accumulation process. The network of pension funds would have significant power in corporate affairs, both because of their shares and their investment policies. The fund network would develop its own cadre of financial specialists and would have reason to assist the tax authorities to monitor and enforce fiscal regulations.[6]

But, it might be objected, is not a fund based on shares vulnerable to the inevitable swings of the market? Dividend income is, in fact, much less volatile than share price, and the networks would count on dividends not share sales for their income. The pension fund network would be encouraged to use dividend revenue to buy corporate and public bonds to diversify their holdings. The network would also have to offer unquoted private companies the option of contributing bonds rather than shares. The networks would be barred from selling the shares they hold – Meidner's approach to social provision is to follow the method of 'de-commodification', in this case means of production. The social fund would, in the first instance, concentrate on building up resources for the future to pay for the sharp increase in social expenditure that will be required by two fundamental processes – the ageing of the population and the increasing need for further education and lifelong learning.

In the end, of course, the social expenditure of the future will have to be paid out of the production of the future, and this means that some future incomes will have to be allocated to this purpose. The share levy approach ensures that *rentier* incomes – returns to capital – will be diverted from wealthy individuals to the network of social funds.

Europe would, of course, be better able to dedicate itself to saving and improving its welfare arrangements and educational provision if it does not allow itself to be dragged into US military exploits. Washington's bellicosity is itself prompted by the desire to distract US citizens from grave social problems, and ballooning inequality, at home. Europe should aspire to a quite different model, both for its own people and in its relations with the rest of the world. Developing some welfare ties at a continental level, binding together old and new members, would help to build the sense of common citizenship which might underpin an independent and progressive foreign policy.

Notes
1 *Wall Steet Journal*, 23 July, 2004.
2 Robin Blackburn, 'Eurodenial', *New Left Review*, No 18, November-December 2003; see also Andrea Boltho, 'What's Wrong with Europe?', *New Left Review*, No 22, July-August 2003
3 The original plan is set out in Rudolf Meidner, *Employee Investment Funds*, London 1978. For an account of the struggles over its implementation see Jonas Pontusson, 'Sweden: the People's Home in Danger', in Perry Anderson and Patrick Camiller, eds. *Mapping the Left In Western Europe*, London 1994.
4 James K. Galbraith, Pedro Conceicao and Pedro Ferreira, 'Inequality and Unemployment in Europe', *New Left Review*, Sept-Oct 1999.
5 Philip Arestis, Kevin McCauley and Malcolm Sawyer, 'An Alternative Stability Pact for the European Union, *Cambridge Journal of Economics*, vol 25, no 1, 2001.
6 Though multinationals have many ways of evading tax through the use of transfer pricing, and the manipulation of allowances, the fiscal authorities, if properly supported by legislators, are far from powerless. For example, they can combat the siphoning off of profits as interest on intra-group loans – 'thin capitalisation' – by using operating profit as the basis for their calculations. See the interesting – if over-optimistic – report by Michael P. Devereux, Rachel Griffith, and Alexander Klemm, 'Why Has the UK Corporation Tax Raised So much Revenue?', Institute of Fiscal Studies, London, February 2004. I look at other technical aspects of 'Meidner-style' levies, including the likely yield, in 'The Pension Gap and How to Fix It', *Challenge*, September-October 2004 and 'How to Rescue a Failing Pension System: the British Case', in *New Political Economy*, December 2004.

The Social State in Europe

Eight theses

André Brie MEP

The author is a well-known member of the European Parliament who represents the Party of Democratic Socialism in Germany. This article forms part of a longer essay on European Social Policy by Dr. Brie, published in the Socialist Renewal series by Spokesman Books (see www.spokesmanbooks.com).

The Keynesian welfare state has been under constant fire since the end of the 1970s. Up until the 1990s, the prevailing pattern was to shrink the social safety net within the established system by cuts in unemployment benefit, pensions, the health service, and the like. Since the mid-1990s, the policy of cuts has been combined with a 'systemic reordering': the partial privatisation of pension systems; the primacy of personal self-provision; restructuring labour market policy in accordance with the philosophy of workfare; the creation of competitively organised educational, post-graduate training, and health markets. It seems that the Keynesian welfare state, in this way, will disappear sooner or later, and yield its place to a competition-oriented market.

The political left in Europe vacillates mainly between the option of an 'adaptation of the social state to the conditions of globalisation' and the 'defence of the achieved'. It tends to be minorities who want to put the social state on a new foundation – in Germany, the pertinent keywords are 'value creation tax', 'citizen and gainfully employed insurance', 'social basic insurance', and so on.[1] Broad, defensive mass protests by trade unions and social movements in Europe including general strikes (Greece 2001, Italy 1994/95, 2002/03, Spain and Portugal 2002, Austria and France 2003, Germany 2003 and 2004) have been able, at times, to delay the continuous social demolition and the liberalisation and privatisation of public goods in the member states of the European Union, but not to stop it. From defence and protest to an alternative is, apparently, a long and arduous endeavour. Nevertheless, we cannot avoid asking ourselves the question: what has to be changed in order to maintain and renew the social state?

Thesis 1

The 'social state class compromise' has only modified the basic asymmetrical distribution of power between capital and labour, it has not structurally dissolved it. The compromise functioned under the good weather conditions of the long post-war upswing, until the beginning of the 1970s, but only as long as high growth rates offered the basis for distributing the increases in output. Thus, in a somewhat abbreviated manner, ran the core of the thesis of *social state illusion*. According to this argument, a fundamental systemic transformation to a socialist society is the only way that holds the long-term promise of overcoming this power asymmetry, and the harmful social consequences linked to it. A mere concentration on 'just compensation' and the transformation of secondary distribution by way of social state instruments promises no permanently stable solution in the interest of the great majority of the population dependent on gainful employment.

This position can call upon Karl Marx: 'If the material conditions of production are the cooperative property of the workers themselves, there also results a distribution of means of consumption different from the one prevailing today. Vulgar socialism (and in turn as part of democracy) took over from the bourgeois economists the observation and treatment of distribution as independent of the mode of production and the presentation of socialism, as if it turned mainly around the question of distribution.' (Marx: *Critique of the Gotha Programme*).[2]

If, together with Marx, we ask ourselves a question about the 'socialist way of production' which, among other things, would rely on a democratic socialisation of the means of production, and would include the moment when we 'produce differently, live differently' – what concretely would we have to imagine? As we know, Marx and Engels shirked this question, because it contradicted their idea of 'scientific socialism'. Instead, they criticised the 'sectarians' and 'Utopians' who imagined another society concretely as unscientific dreamers and handicraft modellers, far removed from reality. Only a field of ruins remains of the 'real socialism' of the Soviet period. Economically, it was not fit for survival; nor was it especially emancipating in socio-political terms. The assumption that a liberated society would result immediately from overcoming capitalist property relations in a certain way (state ownership of the means of production) has proved to be too simplistic. For the rest, there is at this point no developed debate about alternative visions of a socialist society, not even about the old social-democratic demand for 'economic democracy'. What follows practically, therefore, from the call for a 'socialist alternative', which springs from the thesis of 'social state illusion'?

To start with, there is not even a well anchored 'theory construction site'. The anti-globalisation movement is only just starting to think about concepts such as global public goods, new property forms in the 'knowledge society' (free software, 'copyleft'), about participative budgets, and the strengthening of communal democracy ('reclaiming the state'). Usually it does this in a framework which is quite clearly oriented towards 'reform' in the Keynesian sense. Small circles of leftist intellectuals belabour questions of 'market socialism' or 'participative planning' at a high level of abstraction. One can learn quite a few things from such sources, but the debate is at best just starting. It is still far from offering more concrete projects for political and economic strategies, whether in the sense of 'market socialism' or a 'participative economy' (parecon). To develop these approaches further and make them fit for 'daily life' will probably take a long time, and require public and political resonance. This would be part of a serious debate about the future of the social state and conceptions of a 'socialist social state'.[3]

But let us not think that the social state is now a 'mere illusion'. Even in Britain, after the deep cuts of the neo-liberal revolution under Margaret Thatcher, social provision still accounts for about 27% of gross domestic product, which is close to the European Union average. It cannot be killed off as quickly as many right-wing ideologues would wish. Apparently, once a particular course of social development has been taken, it cannot easily be erased. Without the instruments of the Keynesian welfare state, now in the process of being demolished, the social reality and the crisis in Europe would look much more brutal than they currently do. Even though only the secondary distribution has been touched by it, it is an achievement to be defended, and a point of departure for more.

Thesis 2

In 1952, Gerhard Mackenroth, the theoretician of the social state, formulated a fundamental insight: 'that all social expense must always be covered from the popular income of the *current period*.' Whether social protection, social insurance, universal social basic insurance, capital-covered or tax-based mechanism – the sentence holds for everything in equal measure: 'there is no accumulation of funds, no transfer of shares of income as a source of social expense... The problem of national economics cannot be solved or pushed aside by acting according to the principles of an ordinary businessman and insuring private risks. At the national economic level, there does not exist an accumulation of consumption funds which can be consumed when needed, and which can then, in a way, be a welcome addition to the popular income of a later period.'

The financial markets are in no way a miracle weapon for 'saving the social system', as many politician and economists want us to believe. The system of capital coverage is dependent on a permanent rise in productivity and, for example, on financing consumption in old age by restraining the gainfully employed from immediate consumption (thus, on saving).

Individuals may put aside money for tomorrow by saving today. A national economy as a whole cannot do that. It can guarantee social consumption in the future only by real physical and social investment today. The return on a pension fund or life insurance has to be produced in the current period. If this is not possible, the expected increase in value is lost.

Nor does international trade with obligations (for example, pension funds) solve this basic problem. This is because the capital that flows in from abroad (through the purchase of 'German' or 'European' securities) has first to be produced, and is subtracted from the gross domestic product of these countries. This also holds the other way around – one should only think of the glorious idea that European pension funds should invest in Chinese stocks and bonds and the Chinese workers are then supposed to produce 'our pensions'. Whichever way one turns it, one economic truism always holds: *There is no such thing as a free lunch!*

Before it is simply claimed that 'we' can no longer afford the social state, two questions pose themselves:
- How is the popular income currently *produced?* (Karl Marx's core question) and
- How is it *distributed* (the equally justified core question of the old social-democratic workers' movement), so that sufficient social expenditure in the current period can be served out of it?

The economy of Europe no longer grows as rapidly as it did in the 1950s and 1960s, but it is still growing. If we 'save' on social expenditures under these conditions, other social groups may receive a larger share of the national income.

Thesis 3

Many look at the controversy about the social state almost exclusively from the point of view of 'social justice'. This is surely important. At first, however, we have to remember *'It's the economy, stupid!'* In times of high mass unemployment, there is the need first to try to come to terms with the *political economy of the social state.*

Heiner Flassbeck has pronounced a truth at first bitter for the left: 'The conflict over justice, the social safety net and solidarity in society is completely meaningless in times of high and rising unemployment. In such times, any measure that creates 100,000 jobs is considered just; any renunciation of wages, social protection or insurance protection which brings others wages and bread, as solidarity-inspired to the highest degree.'[4]

It is, after all, not an accident that in the last 25 years large parts of the trade unions also believed the general propaganda that every one had to 'tighten their belts' and save from the point of view of the trade unions 'in a socially just way', so that the entrepreneurs, the high income earners, and wealth holders were also just a little bit fleeced. The background to this is the static and continuously high mass unemployment, which apparently cannot be addressed. It can hardly come any better for the executioners of the social state: the general logic of austerity and an apparently necessary flexibility is widely accepted. The dispute is no longer about the economy, but about who, in the name of 'solidarity', has to make what contribution to the general 'saving'.

From the economic point of view, however, the following question has to be asked: when the state as well as private households both restrain their expenditures, in other words 'save', how then should the entrepreneurs (quite independently of who owns them) expand sales and be able again to invest more? If some entrepreneurs now try to improve their situation by constant 'cost reductions' (of wages, wage supplements, and so on), they will only worsen the position of other entrepreneurs and the demand potential of other households. In the round that then follows, the state has less tax income and higher expenditures, because there are more unemployed people. Nothing comes of the envisaged budgetary consolidation and the debt reduction – new holes have to be mended. This cycle is known as the 'debt paradox'. From the point of view of the whole economy, this policy, socially as well as economically, leads to a downward spiral in which, in the end, everybody loses. It is not only socially unjust but also wrong, precisely from the point of view of economic policy. Current popular income stays far below what it could be, and what could be achieved by way of *another economic and financial policy*.

Thesis 4

Keynes clearly pointed to the connections between the economy, distribution, the social state and developed strategies, and how they can be worked to achieve durable 'well-being for all'. In his conception, the social and welfare state was embedded in an expansive macroeconomic policy for full employment, state investment guidance, control of the financial markets, curbing of speculation and a more balanced distribution of income and wealth.

Against this argument, it is today held that such a policy would only have any chance at all under conditions of closed national economies, not under those of 'globalisation'. A series of emerging industrial economies have pursued a more strongly domestically-oriented strategy (for example, Thailand, Malaysia, China, and Argentina after the crash). They have at least shown that they are able to achieve better economic results than those applying the neo-liberal mantras of structural adaptation.[5] For Europe within the European Union, another argument is much more decisive: 'since less than 10% of the gross domestic product of the European Union is exported to non-EU countries, it is no exaggeration to characterise the European Union as a closed economy.' (Kleinknecht/Wengel 1998, p. 641). The medium and small European national state may have become too small to deal with the economic problems, but the European Union as a whole is not.

This also means that social, tax and environmental standards can be regulated at a European level, and thus be withdrawn from global competition. A co-ordinated European tax and financial policy for solid and distributively just financing of the social tasks of the member states, co-ordinated economic policy for strengthened public investments in social infrastructure and environmental structural change, co-ordinated monetary and budgetary policy for the strengthening of the European domestic economy, and the environmentally sound revival of domestic demand — all this can be worth it and lead to full employment.[6] The social state in Europe can thus be maintained and renewed.

Ecologists criticise Keynes' strategy as fixated upon growth. High economic growth increases environmental problems because of the greater consumption of energy and raw materials. This criticism of Keynes, however, is only partly justified: 'The Keynesian long-term strategy (Keynes, 1943), which prognosticated lessening growth (stagnation) for the highly developed national economies, such that it would no longer be possible to achieve full employment on the traditional way of high growth rates, thus then also did not usher in a elaborate new edition of growth stimulating politics, but Keynes recommended already more than half a century ago in the middle of the Second World War (1943!) step-wise reductions in labour time. The argument for this way back to full employment is also supported by the most recent ecological problem discussion: ultimately, any kind of growth harms the economy, so that also in the future, it will be necessary to solve the employment and social problems also without (high) economic growth rates.' (Karl Georg Zinn 2003).

Zinn's proposal of a 'qualitative Keynesianism', at least as a transitional programme in the medium term (20 to 30 years), has some plausibility. In common with Marx and political ecology, it places the changing of 'the exchange of materials with nature' in the foreground: ecological and social restructuring for a sustainable development. At the margins of the trade union and environmental movement, there has already developed a basic framework for a comprehensive, sustainable strategy. The recommended individual tools certainly require discussion, but the fundamental logic of alternative development points in the correct direction.

Ecological innovation on a broad front leads to a multitude of new products and services: solar-hydrogen-economy, fuel cells, drastic energy and resource saving, ecological farming, plant-based chemistry, bionics, ethno-botany, green information technology, mobility and energy services. It will take a while, until new satisfaction levels are reached in this way. Environmental innovation is closely linked with social innovation: eco-efficient services, the extension of social and cultural services, social citizenship rights, rights of economic democracy, education and qualification, a new working-time standard, and 'Useful Work'. The return to high growth rates is not at the centre: rather, a far-reaching dematerialisation of the economy, and the targeted improvement of the living conditions of the majority of the population.

Qualitative Keynesianism thus promotes lasting, ecologically sound and just well-being for all. It is fully compatible with far-reaching eco-socialist conceptions. And it creates an economic environment in which a social state that has been renewed on the basis of solidarity can be embedded.

Thesis 5

Then there is the question of the 'demographic challenge'. On present trends, by the year 2050, the proportion of people in Europe who are aged over 65 will have doubled; after that the population will begin to shrink significantly. This is seen only as a cost problem. The demographic changes will be met by cuts in pensions and health systems, and the instruction to make 'more private provision'.

But the 'cost problem' of an ageing and shrinking population can be met comparatively easily. By maintaining the average growth in productivity of the past 100 years, Europe will be in a position to sustain welfare even with a shrinking proportion of the population gainfully employed, and so guarantee adequate material security for both young and old equally. There is no doubt that the tax and contribution basis for financing social security systems for the elderly has to be broadened, and income and wealth differentials have to be reduced more sharply.

The political mainstream, however, does not ask the really important questions: how do work and living conditions have to be changed so that people can stay healthy and happy in gainful employment, and can remain so when they reach retirement age? Which social, educational and other infrastructures are needed in a society where the proportion of elderly and older people continues to increase over several decades? And how should the life conditions of children and young people be designed, so that they can develop in an all-round way?

For the future, we must seek deceleration, sufficiency, distributive justice, health promotion and individual freedom, instead of more inequality, market constraint, ever more stress, and entrepreneurial 'flexibility'. The solution to the demographic question requires more social provision and a better social state, in parallel to the necessary changes in work and economic life.

Thesis 6

In light of the diversity of welfare state traditions in the European Union, the debate about a renewal of the social state in Europe can be maintained only at the level of guiding images and functions, which the social security systems are thus supposed to fulfil.

Socialist policy stands for a social state that guarantees social citizenship rights materially by way of universal and unconditional services in the framework of a public all-encompassing insurance.[7] Health, education, protection against social risks, and so on have to be considered as *public goods*, which should be withdrawn from market compulsion and market forces. From there, as a guiding vision for the renewal of the social security systems, there follows the concept of a people's or citizens' insurance. Contribution requirements (whether as taxes or social contributions) and claims for services tie in with *inhabitant status,* and no longer exclusively with gainful employment, as was the case in the conservative-corporatist welfare state.

The financing of the tasks of the social state is to be borne by all inhabitants (female and male) and businesses according to their financial capability. Thus, the basis of contribution will be broadened, and the principle of solidarity-based redistribution strengthened. There exists a considerable spectrum of proposals on how this general guiding image is to be implemented concretely. In the context of the German Federal Republic, some propose to finance social security generally by way of a value-creation tax. Thus, part of the value created would be taken out of the conflict over primary distribution (between capital and labour) and reserved exclusively to finance social-state tasks. Others envisage replacing the employers' contribution to social insurance by a value-creation tax.

Still others want to extend the contribution base of the social security system (for example, to self-employed people, civil servants, housewives, and so on), as well as with respect to the inclusion of other kinds of income (for example, rent, interest and capital returns). In this context, reference is often made to already existing national state models of a 'citizen insurance' (for example, health insurance in Austria, pension insurance in Switzerland). The strengths and weaknesses as well as the consequences of the respective 'models' are tied predominantly to the national context, and should be evaluated in this framework. They all have in common that they imply a completely different direction for social state renewal than the 'social reforms' now being implemented in the member states, and the current socio-political guiding vision at the level of the European Union.

Socialist politics strives for comprehensive equality between women and men. At odds with this are the social concepts of normality, which are imbued with the patriarchal image of the male head of the household and which still characterise most social states in the European Union. The renewal of the social state has to overcome the multiple disadvantages of women and insist on egalitarian patterns of gainful employment: equal payment for work of equal value, equal career opportunities, shorter work times and access to protected part-time work for both sexes. Independent tax and social systems can be taken up on this basis; that is, the abolition of the social and tax policy privileges of the 'housewife marriage' and the 'marital partnership'. Whether people live together with or without a marriage certificate is their affair. The tax and social system should not favour one or the other arrangement.

Thus, the advantages enjoyed by the married couple have to be completely removed from family policy. There remains the simple sentence: family is where there are children. In this respect, the renewal of the social state has to be above all service-oriented: an area-wide extension of public child-care centres, which makes possible the compatibility of family and profession. A targeted financial support of households with children ('family burden compensation') is to be borne in solidarity by the whole community, in the form of tax-financed basic child allowances.

Socialist policy strives for basic social security, which prevents poverty and enables equal participation in social well-being (participative justice). Security in old age is to be achieved by solidarity-based, redistributive public systems. It must fulfil two functions: basic social security in old age (as basic security for all) and maintenance of adequate living standards (performance justice). Periods of child-rearing, caring for elderly relatives, and basic and post-graduate training, as well as phases of unemployment and sickness have to be adequately taken into account. The health system including long-term care has to be financed on the basis of solidarity (an income-proportional and thereby redistributive contribution assessment), and must provide qualitatively high-level services to all independent of their income. A 'citizen insurance system' in this context allows a more targeted prevention policy (and thereby opens considerable cost-reduction potentials) than a market-economy dismembered health system. Unemployment support has to remain an unconditional social legal claim, guarantee freedom of choice of occupation, and uphold and renew already acquired qualifications.

The repair of all three pillars of social protection — care for the elderly, health care, and gainful employment — requires a new policy of full employment and social redistribution (compare Thesis 4). Without this, an egalitarian renewal of the social state will not succeed.

Thesis 7

In the European Union, the social state is primarily developed at the level of the national state, and this in very different ways. In accordance with the dogma of strengthening 'competitiveness', a harsh regime of competition between the national social states has been established. The member states are constantly tempted to achieve a competitive edge by demolishing social benefits. Thus, the question at the European level is, first of all, to prevent increased social dumping in the extended European Union.

Agreement on a social stability pact is necessary to achieve this goal. This builds on the simple fact that there exists a very close connection between the economic development of a country (measured as gross domestic product per head), and its social performance quota (the share of all social expenditure in gross domestic product).

In the framework of a social stability pact, the social performance quotas of the 25 European Union member states would first be recorded and countries with similar quotas put together in a group ('corridor'). A downward departure from the initial value would entail a consultation procedure for the countries concerned and, if necessary, sanctions. In this way, social development would be coupled to economic development. The more weakly developed national economies in the European Union would not be over-taxed by this form of social policy regulation. The more they gained in economic development, the more their social performance quotas would approach those in the rest of the European Union. The economically stronger member countries would thus have their way barred to social dumping (under average social benefit quotas in relation to their income level).

The European Union can and must do considerably more than just prevent social dumping. In the future it must set binding, quantitative and qualitative social policy tasks: for example, for the improvement of health insurance, for the minimal level of social protection, for European minimum wage standards, for overcoming poverty, social exclusion, homelessness and illiteracy. It has to be possible, within this framework, to commit the member states to concrete programmes whose implementation will be continually analysed and controlled. The European Union can supplement these programmes by European promotion. Thus, European social policy would begin to have an independent effect, beyond merely gathering information, agreeing indicators and comparing 'best practices'.

In the perspective of social policy, there is also the question of the 'finality of European integration' – towards which goal should it ultimately strive? Within the framework of a federal or confederated European Union, don't we also need a European social union ('Social State European Union'), as was demanded by the anti-fascist movements in Europe after the Second World War? Is it sensible to lay down, at the European level, unified norms for standards of service, levels of benefits, and additional entitlements, as well as adaptations of rules? Core ingredients of social security, for example, might be basic social security, old age and invalidity pensions, unemployment support, family benefits, and health services. In this way, the manifold practical problems that have until now beset the 'coordination of social protection systems' in the areas of free mobility and freedom of residence of persons, would resolve themselves.

The key to such a solution lies in choosing relative reference parameters: for example, as far as a European basic social security is concerned, there should be a benefit level of 60% of the national average income of the member state, in which a person chooses to reside. Thus, there would be no incentive to 'social tourism' – for example, by taking along the relatively generous basic social protection provided in the Netherlands when settling in regions with low living costs such as Apulia or Extremadura if, for instance, the national state social insurance were to be made 'transportable' all over Europe. The economic performance of the respective member state of residence would be duly taken into account by the choice of relative reference parameters.

Today, this debate still sounds like the distant music of the future. But if one wants to prevent the increased 'Europe-wide patient mobility' that is presently being discussed and opens the way to a European Union domestic market in health services, which would gradually undermine the solidarity-based health systems of the national states that have already been severely hit by the recent 'health reforms', then one also has to think about European solutions.

Thesis 8

What are the social and political forces that can produce a dynamic in the direction of a social Europe?

Under present conditions, these are still relative minorities: they are the trade unions, acting up now mainly at the level of the nation state, which are opposed to social demolition; the social movements coming together in the European Social Forum (ESF), voluntary organisations and initiatives: and the European left-wing parties as well as minority tendencies in the European Greens and Social Democrats.

The European Social Forum undoubtedly makes an important contribution to creating a European democratic political public – alongside the formations of European political parties and foundations as well as existing European associations and networks. With the European days of action by the European Trade Union Confederation (ETUC) and the social movements on April 2 and 3, 2004, perhaps a beginning was made to going beyond resistance to social state demolition at the national state level to a discussion about a common European perspective and capability for action.

In this respect, nobody should be taken in by the illusion that it might be possible to compensate, at a European level, for defeats at the local, regional or national levels. The fight for a social Europe must rather be viewed as an initiative within a political system of several levels. In this respect, the social state, public services, and existing public provision can be defended at the local, regional and national levels. But if it is not possible to back up this policy with a European dimension (the social stability pact, Social Union), these efforts are always structurally on the defensive. The European Union's economic policy, its growth and stability pact, and its policy of deregulation in the domestic market all continuously erode progress. Without the perspective of a turn in this developmental logic also at the European level, these struggles remain precarious and incomplete.

If we succeed in building up a European dimension of resistance against the demolition of the social state, this in turn can have positive feedback for the activities in the same direction at the national, regional and local levels. After all, nothing is more inspiring than to discover common concerns with a multitude of sympathetic minds and to see one's own activities reinforced and supported by those of others. In the present phase, the issue will mainly be whether, by common European discussion and activities, a minimum consensus can emerge between the participants concerning core elements in the renewal of the social state, which then develops persuasive influence on social majorities. When the widespread belief that 'there is no alternative' is for the first time seriously challenged, then it will become possible to gradually overcome the present defensive situation.

Translated by Carla Krüger
References available on request to elfeuro@compuserve.com

Notes
1 Concerning the concept of financing social insurance by way of a value creation tax in Germany, compare Christen/Kahrs/Weise 2000. The concepts of the German green and alternative Left, from the 1980s and 1990s, concerning the 'citizens and gainfully employed insurance' and the 'social basic insurance' have received a radical reinterpretation in the Agenda 2010 and the Rürup Commission. Compare Bartelheimer 2003 and Kreutz 2003.
2 Marx by the way even declined to speak about a 'social question', which lies at the basis of the later discourse about the social state: 'In the stead of the existing class struggle, there enters a newspaper writer phrase – the "social question", whose "solution" one "prepares the ground for". Instead of from the revolutionary transformation process of society the "socialist organisation of total labour" "emerges" from the "state help" that the state gives to productive cooperatives, which IT, not the worker, "calls into being". This is worthy of the imagination of Lassalle that one can with state obligations build a new society just as well as a new railroad!' (Marx: *Critique of the Gotha Programme*)
3 Marx has addressed the latter question in the criticism of the Gotha Programme. He

referred to the fact that from the 'products of labour' there after all also had to be formed 'funds for those incapable of working', for 'common needs' such as schools and health institutions as well as 'insurance against accidents and disturbances'.

4 Flassbeck, Heiner (2003): Wie Deutschland wirtschaftlich ruiniert wurde, Ein Bericht aus dem Jahr 2010 (How Germany was ruined economically, A Report from the year 2010), in: *Blätter für deutsche und internationale Politik* 8/2003, pp. 955-965.

5 My reference pertains not only to the quantitative economic results (increase in the GDP and the national popular income), with which the mainstream economists are after all mainly concerned in their argumentation. That the social position of people, the income distribution, the income pollution etc. in these countries are anything else but desirable, stands on another leaf, and this can also only be changed by different social relationships of forces and corresponding political conceptions in these countries themselves.

6 More concrete proposals for such policies I have submitted some time ago (compare Brie/Dräger 2001, Brie 2002). Much of it can also be found in the programme of the PDS for the European elections.

7 The same is also claimed by the Scandinavian social-democratic welfare state model; yet, social democracy in Sweden has also introduced its reconstruction. However, it should still be stressed that the Scandinavian model in the EU comparison economically as well as socially still reaches better results than the others (comp. Corsi/Orsini 2001).

Empire in Africa

Michael Barratt Brown

Michael Barratt Brown is the author of Africa's Choices *(Penguin Books). This article is based on a paper prepared for the Boston Social Forum, which met in July 2004.*

Governments in the United States, Britain and France have recently been showing a new interest in the African continent. Mr Bush, Mr Blair and M.Chirac have all made visits to African countries within the last two years. Mr Blair made much of his concern for Africa's problems in his speech to the Labour Party Conference in 2002, and has recently spoken in favour of military intervention in the Sudan.

Nobody intervened in the genocide in Rwanda. Why in the Sudan? Was it possible that this was a belated recognition of the crisis of Africa's indebtedness to Western banks, further instigated by horror at the humanitarian disasters in Rwanda as in Sierra Leone, the Congo and most recently in Ethiopia? Might something be done to help to treat the AIDS epidemic, cancel the debts and establish fairer trading relations between the rich developed countries' consumers and Africa's poorest producers. I doubt it. Sudan has the most recently developed oil production in Africa piped out to Port Sudan. Controlling the government of Sudan becomes a crucial interest of the great powers, not least of the Americans, because it is the French and the Chinese who have major interests in developing Sudanese oil.

It has become increasingly clear – and a recent article in *Le Monde Diplomatique** has spelt out the horrid truth – that the real aim of western Governments is to align African governments with new imperial policies and, in particular, to establish control over Africa's rich mineral resources – and all this done in the name of the battle against terrorism. This has, of course, been a real issue since the 1998 attacks claimed for Al Qaeda on US embassies in Nairobi and Dar es Salaam, to which the most inappropriate bombing of a pharmaceutical plant in Sudan was Clinton's response. The failure of US intervention in Somalia is not forgotten. Since 1997, quite large scale US military assistance and training schemes have been launched in Algeria, Morocco, Chad, Mauritania, Mali, Niger, Egypt and Kenya, with a naval presence in the Gulf of Guinea and the Red Sea, and a base proposed in Sao Tomé. In the years 1998-2002, Egypt was the largest recipient of US arms, larger even than Israel, Saudi Arabia and Turkey.

Already in the mid 1990s, the US State Department created an African Crisis Response Initiative (ACRI) to provide training for peace-keeping and humanitarian aid, in effect to modernise local armed forces and equip them with American arms to respond to emerging terrorism. ACRI's coordinator is Col. Nestor Pino-Marina, a Cuban exile, who took part in the failed US landing in the Bay of Pigs in 1961, in the Vietnam campaign and in clandestine operations with the Contras in Nicaragua in the 1990s. Between 1997 and 2000, ACRI organised training for local army battalions in Senegal, Uganda, Malawi, Mali, Ghana, Benin and Côte d'Ivoire. According to Colonel Nestor Pino-Marina, 'accepted doctrine commonly used in Nato is being absorbed'. Following upon the events of 9/11, the Bush government acted. In spring 2002, ACRI was reorganised by the Pentagon into ACOTA – African Contingency Operations Training Assistance – and offensive training was added to training for peace-keeping and humanitarian aid. In May 2003, Mali hosted a seminar on combating terrorism in the region, attended by delegates from Algeria, Chad, Mali, Mauritania, Morocco, Niger, Nigeria and Senegal, and also by representatives from Germany and France.

Two months later in July 2003, President Bush, in his first foray outside of America, made an African tour comprising visits to Senegal, Nigeria, Botswana, Uganda and South Africa. His message was that 'we will not allow terrorists to threaten African people, or to use Africa as a base to threaten the world'. Besides ACOTA, 44 African countries have been taking part in a programme organised by the Pentagon especially for officers (International Military Education and Training – IMET), at a cost of $11 million in 2003. Botswana, Ethiopia, Ghana, Kenya, Nigeria, Senegal and South Africa have been involved. ACOTA is linked to the training centres of the Joint Arms Training System (JCATS), run by Military Professional Resources Inc (MPRI), which uses sophisticated software to mimic battle conditions. Colonel Victor Nelson, a former US military attaché to Nigeria, who runs the Sahel initiative, claims that this is an inexpensive way of providing officer training. Nigeria is the first African country to have such a centre at Abuja.

All this activity led up to a meeting on March 23-24, 2004 at the US European Command (US-Eucom) headquarters at Stuttgart in Germany. Chiefs of Staff took part from Chad, Mali, Mauritania, Morocco, Niger, Senegal and Tunisia. Defence against terrorists who might attack the oil fields of North Africa and those of the Gulf of Guinea was the subject of the meeting. One particular group accused of terrorist activity in the region of the Sahel, between the Maghreb and Sub-Saharan Africa, is the Salafist Group for Preaching and Combat (GSPC). It is suspected of having links with Al Qaeda. Colonel

Nelson, who oversees the programme of the US Defense Department's Office of International Security Affairs (PSI), explained that the 'PSI was an important tool in the war on terrorism and has gone a long way to open doors and establish relationships notably between Algeria, Mali, Niger and Chad...If you squeeze the terrorists in Afghanistan, Pakistan, Iraq and other places, they will find new places to operate, and one of those places is the Sahel/Maghreb'.

This is a region which has historically been under French influence. The people speak French and France still has military bases in one-time French colonies – Senegal, Côte d'Ivoire, Chad, Central African Republic, Gabon, Madagascar, Mauritius and Djibouti. Increasing US interest might be expected to cause some friction, especially in Djibouti, where the United States now has a permanent base near to the French base. This tiny state on the edge of a desert, one of the poorest places in the world, happens to be across from the maritime zone where a quarter of the world's oil passes through, and therefore of great strategic importance, which has been enhanced by the development of oil production in the Sudan and the use of Port Sudan just up the coast from Djibouti. General Charles Wald, the US-Eucom deputy commander, who travelled in March 2004 to Algeria, Morocco, Nigeria, Angola, South Africa, Namibia, Gabon, Sao Tomé, Ghana, Niger and Tunisia, commented that 'the US and France had many common interests.'

Their chief common interest is oil. Much of Africa's oil lies in or under or off shore from what were once French colonies – Algeria, Morocco, Gabon, Congo, Côte d'Ivoire, Equatorial Guinea, Cameroun. French companies alongside of US and British companies operate concessions.

African oil has become increasingly important in the last decades and now ranks second only to the Middle East, supplying about 15% of the world's oil (see Appendix). Troubles in the Middle East and the declining reserves in the United States and in Europe have given to these African reserves their especial importance. Establishing and maintaining imperial interests have become essential once more. Oil pipelines and installations are prime targets for terrorist attack. Their protection cannot be left to corrupt and ill-prepared local élites.

In the arms for oil business there is a symbiosis between the giant arms companies of the United States and the United Kingdom and the giant oil companies. Protecting their oil fields from sabotage requires the importation of arms by the oil producers. The sale of arms is most easily financed by payment with oil, sometimes even with barter deals. The chief recipients of international arms transfers are the oil producing states, Saudi Arabia in particular. Western governments have not been above selling arms simultaneously to warring oil producers, as in the case of the Iran-Iraq war, and of supporting with arms and then attacking an oil state, as in the case of Saddam Hussein's Iraq. There is much evidence to show that a small cabal in each western state is responsible for encouraging the arms for oil business.

African states suffer like other Developing Countries from their inheritance of an artificial economy of trade relations established under colonial rule. In each colony production of two or three primary commodities was established for export to the colonial power, and in exchange manufactures were imported. Thus in the case of the oil producing countries, oil exports make up some 80% to 100% of all trade; in the case of the coffee, tea and cocoa producers dependency on these exports accounts for 50% to 60% of all trade; in the case of the cotton and tobacco producers the proportion ranges from 30% to 60%. The élites which rule in these countries are closely associated with the main export earning commodity. Control of mineral ore production through state ownership of plant and other operations gives the same privileges to a ruling élite in mineral producing countries. This makes African governments easily susceptible to the influence of the consumer countries, i.e. the ex-colonial powers, and in particular to the giant companies which buy the minerals. Selling arms and training armies has become part of the deal, which the United States and the one-time colonial powers negotiate.

There has recently been some recovery in world commodity prices – not only in oil prices as the result of the Iraq war, but also in the prices of mineral ores and metals. From a level of the upper 80s these rose to 100 in 1994 and 108 in 2003. The explanation appears to be large-scale Chinese buying. Africa is still a relatively small world producer of minerals (see Appendix). The exception lies in certain exotic ores. Zaire and Zambia have 50% of world cobalt reserves and South Africa and Zimbabwe some 90% of chrome reserves and South Africa has also 90% of the reserves of the platinum group of metals. These together with uranium in Namibia and gold and diamonds in southern Africa can well account for the renewed interest of the United States in this neglected and much damaged continent.

US interest in controlling the oil in Sudan is also driven by Chinese as well as French competition. We should not be fooled by the claims that rescuing Darfur with an all-African force is once more 'humanitarian intervention'. Such a force will be under ultimate US command and using US arms, and having 'absorbed Nato military doctrine' with its command centre at Abuja, and protected from the military bases in Sao Tomé and Djibouti.

We have seen all this before. Intervention in Yugoslavia led to the establishment of the largest US military base outside the United States, Camp Bondsteel in Kosovo, just north of the Albanian port of Vlores. This just where it is planned for the proposed trans-Balkan pipeline through Bulgaria and Macedonia, both minions of the United States, to end, and give deep water anchorage for the very largest 300,000 tonne tankers, bringing oil from the newly developed oil fields entering the Black Sea for export to the United States.

References available on request.

* *Le Monde Diplomatique,* English edition, 08.07.04, pp.8-9

APPENDIX

AFRICA'S SHARES OF WORLD MINERAL EXPORTS, 1970-2000
(all figures in $billions)

All Non-Fuel Minerals

Country	Commodities	1970	1980	1990	2000
World	all non-fuel	23.5	96.8	126.9	176.3
S.Africa	gold, chrome, platinum	0.4	2.0	2.5	5.3
Developing Africa	(as below)	2.6	6.5	6.2	3.8
Morocco	fertiliser	0.2	0.4	0.6	0.7
Zaire	copper, cobalt	0.6	0.7	0.7	0.2
Zambia	copper, cobalt	1.0	1.4	1.2	0.5
Guinea	bauxite	–	0.5	0.6	0.4
Niger	uranium	–	0.5	0.2	0.1
Zimbabwe	chrome, nickel	0.2	0.3	0.2	0.2
Ghana	gold, aluminium manganese	–	0.3	0.3	0.2
Liberia	iron ore	0.2	0.3	–	–
Namibia	uranium, silver, lead diamonds	0.1	0.2	0.4	0.1
Botswana	diamonds	–	0.1	0.2	0.2

Mineral fuels

Country	Commodities	1970	1980	1990	2000
World	all fuel	28.2	482	370	661
S. Africa		0.1	1.0	1.5	2.0
Developing Africa		4.0	70.4	44.3	73.6
Nigeria		0.7	24.3	13.3	20.0
Algeria		0.1	15.4	10.5	21.1
Libya		2.3	21.9	10.7	13.2
Angola		–	1.5	3.7	7.1
Gabon		–	1.2	1.7	2.5
Congo		–	0.4	1.0	2.4
Egypt		–	2.0	0.8	1.7
Sudan		–	–	0.3	1.4
Cote d'Ivoire		–	–	0.4	0.7
Equit. Guinea		–	–	–	1.1
Cameroon		–	0.4	1.0	0.6
Morocco		–	–	0.2	0.3

Sources: *UNCTAD Commodity Yearbook, 2003*, Tables 1.10 and 1.12 and UNCTAD *Handbook of Statistics*, Table 4.20

THE BERTRAND RUSSELL PEACE FOUNDATION
PEACE DOSSIER

DETENTION IN AFGHANISTAN AND GUANTANAMO BAY

Statement of Shafiq Rasul, Asif Iqbal and Rhuhel Ahmed

We referred to the cases of Feroz Abbasi and and Moazzam Begg, two British citizens still detained at Guantanamo Bay, in Dark Times *(Spokesman 81). Subsequently, Jamal al –Harith, another British citizen, shed some light on the conditions in the camps, and the practices and abuses there, when he was released in March 2004. This was prior to the circulation of the pictures of torture at Abu Ghraib in Iraq, in April 2004, which shocked the world.*

Now there is a comprehensive statement entitled 'Detention in Afghanistan and Guantanamo Bay', by Shafiq Rasul, Asif Iqbal and Rhuhel Ahmed, who all come from Tipton in the West Midlands of England. These three men were also released from Guantanamo in March. The Statement has been compiled with their lawyers, Birnberg Peirce & Partners, and was released in the United States on 4 August 2004. In the words of the introductory paragraphs, 'This statement jointly made by them constitutes an attempt to set out details of their treatment at the hands of UK and US military personnel and civilian authorities during the time of their detention in Kandahar in Afghanistan in late December 2001 and throughout their time in American custody in Guantanamo Bay Cuba. This statement is a composite of the experiences of all three. They are referred to throughout by their first names for brevity. There is far more that could be said by each, but that task is an open-ended one. They have tried to include the main features.'

We reprint below an excerpt from the closing section of the Statement that treats on 'the state of some other prisoners' who endured mistreatments of diverse kinds and are still held at Guantanamo. Currently 585 people remain there, including four Britons as well as four British residents. Campaigns for their release continue.

Shafiq Rasul, Asif Iqbal and Ruhal Ahmed have set out the degradation they and their colleagues of many nationalities suffered: shackling in a bent position to a ring in the floor for hours or days, isolation for weeks or months, being held naked, kept in freezing air conditioning, sleep deprivation, near-starvation, imposed injections, forced shaving of hair and beard, withholding of family mail, refusal of medical attention, beatings, interrogations, psychological torture to force false confessions or false testimony against others, being confronted with confessions they never made, sexual humiliation, being shown pornographic photos and videos.

They themselves had undergone extraordinary and terrifying experiences even before they arrived in Cuba. All three were detained in Northern Afghanistan in November 2001 by forces loyal to General Dostum, as their Statement reveals: 'According to information all three were given later, there were US forces present at the point they were packed into containers together with almost 200 others. Asif became unconscious and awoke to find that in an attempt to allow air into the containers Dostum's forces had fired machine guns into the sides of the containers. Asif was struck in the arm by a bullet as a result. The journey to Sherbegan took nearly 18 hours and the containers were not opened until they reached the prison. All three men remained in the containers amongst the dead and dying throughout this time. Asif reports that to get water he had to lick the side of the container or wipe a cloth on the top of the container where the condensation had collected and squeeze the drips of water into his mouth. On arrival at Sherbegan of the 200 originally in the container only 20 were alive, some of them seriously injured.' Some of the horrors of that transportation were also recorded by the film producer, Jamie Doran, in 'Massacre at Mazar' (see Spokesman 77).

Whilst at Sherbegan, the men were beaten. Two weeks later, Mr Iqbal and Mr Rasul were flown from Kandahar to Cuba, to be followed a month later by Mr Ahmed. Before their removal, they were hooded and forced to strip, then left naked and subjected to 'cavity' searches. On arrival in Cuba, they feared for their lives as guards told them 'Nobody knows you're here, all they know is that you're missing and we could kill you and no one would know.' Mr Iqbal believes the authorities deliberately fostered mental anguish – 'they had thought carefully about the best way to punish me and break me.'

'We had the impression that at the beginning things were not carefully planned, but a point came at which you could notice things changing. That appeared to be after Gen Miller [arrived] around the end of 2002,' said Mr Rasul. 'That is when short-shackling [when detainees are chained into a squatting position] started, loud music playing in interrogation, shaving beards and hair, putting people in cells naked, taking away people's 'comfort' items [eg towels] ... moving some people every two hours, depriving them of sleep, the use of a/c [air-conditioned, cold] air. Before, when people would be put into blocks for isolation, they would seem to stay for not more than a month. After he came, people would be kept there for months and months and months.'

British officials made repeated visits to Guantanamo to question Britons who had been subjected to ill-treatment by US personnel. Consular officials, who visited at least six times, were supposed to ensure the welfare of the Britons, yet they were always accompanied by MI5 officers. Mr Iqbal says that the embassy official once acted like 'a third interrogator', asking him not about his welfare, but about other matters. British officials saw all three men within three days of their arrival in Cuba. Mr Rasul says he was interviewed under armed guard by someone who said he was from the British embassy in Washington and someone from MI5. He said: 'The MI5 officer told me in no uncertain terms that if I did not cooperate they could make life very difficult for me.' He was told if he admitted going to Afghanistan for jihad, he could return to England. Mr Rasul says he was interviewed twice by MI5 in Camp X-ray, and Mr Ahmed once. Mr Iqbal says British intelligence questioned him four times over three months. His first interrogation by MI5 lasted between six and eight hours. Mr Iqbal 'remembers clearly' that, on one occasion, the official wrote down his list of grievances for the first time. These included infections he was suffering from untreated wounds caused by iron leg shackles; being led naked to and from the showers; poor food; disrespect shown to their religion; and sleep deprivation. The complaint ran to two pages. Mr Rasul says he complained to a British embassy official called Martin, telling him that he had been kept in isolation for three months. Again, nothing seemed to happen. The report concludes: 'It was very clear to all three that MI5 was content to benefit from the effect of the isolation, sleep deprivation and other forms of acutely painful and degrading treatment, including short shackling.'

Lawyer Gareth Peirce said the report showed Britain's complicity in the human rights abuses at Guantanamo. As she told The Guardian, 'The [British government] attitude displayed the hypocrisy of the public face in the UK saying we're doing all we can and the private face there in Guantanamo involved up to their elbows in the oppression.'

There have been 'several hundred' suicide attempts at Guantanamo, many more than suggested in official accounts, according to the Statement. Camp authorities recorded 32 attempts by prisoners to kill themselves before they stopped counting them and created a new category of 'manipulative self-injurious behaviour', for which figures are not disclosed. But the report suggests that attempted suicides are just the tip of the iceberg. It describes in vivid detail the deteriorating mental health of prisoners, including Britons, and alleges that guards have assaulted men who have serious health problems. 'For at least 50 of those their behaviour is so disturbed as to show that they are no longer capable of rational thought or behaviour ... It is something that only a small child or animal might behave like ... These people were obviously seriously ill and yet we understand [from the military police] that they still get interrogated, and if they say someone is from al-Qaida then that information is used.' The excerpt from the three men's Statement follows:

* * *

A few prisoners only are mentioned here.

Jamil el-Banna and Bisher al-Rawi

Asif says he was in Mike block in Camp Delta next to Suwad Al Madini (a Saudi national whose wife is British and whose children are British, also known as

Shakir ...). He recollects, 'A large number of the men were brought into the block from isolation. I believe they came in February 2003 having spent a month in isolation in Guantanamo Bay after they arrived. Abu Ennis, Jamil el-Banna, was put in the cell next to me. Given that he had been in isolation for a month and before that in Bagram Airbase (and before that I understood in Gambia), he was still coping but quite soon after he began to deteriorate. I didn't talk to him much about the Gambia but knew he'd gone there to set up a business. He said that Bagram was very rough. When he arrived at Guantanamo he had very little facial or head hair which he said had all been shaved off in Bagram Airbase. He said that he had been forced to walk around naked, coming and going from the showers, having to parade past American soldiers or guards including women who would laugh at everyone who was put in the same position. When he arrived at Guantanamo his English was not good and still is not good. Bisher al-Rawi was placed on the same row of cells and he used to translate for him. El-Banna was in constant pain from his joints because he suffered from rheumatism and he was diabetic. He told them repeatedly that he was diabetic and they would not believe him.'

'They used to come and take his blood and say that there was nothing wrong with him. Bisher al-Rawi also told them that el-Banna was not well. When you come new they come and take your blood.' (Shafiq recollects that they were told by the guards and by the medical officers who were military, that costs were being cut in respect of food and medicine. They said that the cost of the military personnel was going up and that meant that they had to cut costs in other ways which included food for the prisoners and medical care for the prisoners.

'It was very noticeable by the time we left that the quality of food and the amount of food had gone down. The food had been particularly bad at the beginning. It had improved slightly during the time we were there, but used to noticeably improve just before there was a visit from the Foreign Office.'

(During the first Ramadan Asif recollects they were fasting, obviously. However they would only be provided with two meals a day and those were drastically reduced amounts like four teaspoonfuls of rice. 'We were under the firm impression during the first Ramadan that it was part of a policy to stop us fasting and to cause us to abandon our religious practices. When Ramadan finished the food went back up to normal levels and therefore it was very obvious that it was designed to put pressure on us to stop fasting, which also the doctors and the guards were telling us to stop. The guards served us the food who had been told (they told us this) that they were under orders to give us that much food from their superior officers. When asked after Ramadan why we were back to normal sized rations we were told that the General had ordered that now.')

'It was very clear that el-Banna was devoted to his family. He had photographs of his children including his new daughter. These had come in through the Red Cross. I can recollect one day when the interrogator came to visit him in the block. When she visited him in the block he showed her the pictures of his children and started crying and she said to him we're trying to get you out of here (this was an American interrogator), we know you're an innocent man. I could see as the months went by,' says Asif, 'that he was worrying more and more and that this was having an effect on his mental health. He constantly talked about his children and who would look after them.' (Asif and Shafiq both comment that the repeated questions for Jamil el-Banna whom they questioned less than they questioned Bisher al-Rawi, concerned Abu Qatada and where he was. In the light of the fact that Abu Qatada is known to have been arrested in England in late 2002, it seems extraordinary that this was a question that the Americans were asking.)

Shafiq says that to his knowledge during the time that el-Banna was in Guantanamo he lost about 40 kilos in weight. He started off as someone quite bulky and became someone very, very thin. Asif is aware that el-Banna found it almost impossible to eat the food that was provided. What was provided was a meal packet. 'The meal packets were what we could eat. We were told they cost $7 each and consisted of a main meal, pasta and Alfredo sauce, pasta and vegetables in tomato sauce, black bean burrito, cheese tortellini. The soldiers said that they were inedible, that they wouldn't eat them, but to us they were much much better than what we had before. There were more calories in them and they were more filling. They weren't nice but we felt fuller. Some of these packages were marked to show they were over 12 years old. But then they stopped them around July 2003 and we were told by the guards that they cost too much. (However, a brand new cafeteria was built for the guards. At that point we were told that they had ice cream added to their menu.) el-Banna could manage to eat the packaged meals (called MRE), but he couldn't eat anything else. When they stopped giving those el-Banna couldn't manage to eat anything else. He told the doctors but the General said no one could have these prepackaged meals anymore and he couldn't eat what was on offer. We're completely sure that for the three weeks before we left he wasn't able to eat at all. Eventually we are aware that they put Bisher al-Rawi next to him (they had been separated) to try to keep him going mentally and physically. We would say that mentally basically he's finished. The last thing we heard about him this year before we came back to England was that when he went to interrogation they told him that he was going to be sent back to Jordan and he was extremely scared of that prospect. We knew that he'd been living in England for about ten years and was a refugee and that his whole life was in England and his wife and children. They were clearly the centre of his whole existence and all he ever really thought about. The prospect of being sent to Jordan meant to him the end of his life. He knew that the would be tortured or killed there.'

Bisher al-Rawi

Asif and Shafiq both remember that he was taken for a lie detector test about two weeks after he arrived from isolation in Guantanamo Bay (about six weeks after he got to Cuba), and was told that he'd passed it. He was put up to Level 1, the highest level (when Shafiq was there) but then 'for reasons we don't know and after he'd passed his lie detector test we suddenly heard the he was in isolation and the "privileges" that he'd been given like magazines were taken away as was everything else. We asked him later on when we saw him why he'd been put in isolation and he had no idea. They kept saying to him that he knew more than he was saying.

Bisher al-Rawi had an armband on saying "Iraq" and Jamil el-Banna has an armband on saying "Jordan", even though both of them lived in England.

When Bisher was put in isolation they shaved his head and beard. We know that Bisher was interrogated probably more than 50 times (unlike el-Banna who was probably not interrogated more than about five times). We don't know the exact reasons why Bisher al-Rawi's hair and beard were shaved off but we know that what used to happen to others would by that if you said you didn't want to go to interrogation you would be forcibly taken out of the cell by the ERF team. You would be pepper-sprayed in the face which would knock you to the floor as you couldn't breathe or see and your eyes would be subject to burning pain. Five of them would come in with a shield and smack you and knock you down and jump on you, hold you down and put chains on you. And then you would be taken outside where there would already be a person with clippers who would forcibly shave your hair and beard. Interrogators gave the order for that to be done; the only way in which this would be triggered would be if you were in some way resisting interrogation, in some way showing that you didn't want to be interrogated. Or if during interrogation you were non-cooperative then it could happen as well.

(It was our view that they were looking for vulnerabilities all the time and that the people who seemed most comfortable having a beard or most used to it, those were the ones that they would shave it off. We think with the three of us that they thought we would not be so affected if it happened to us. They would watch how you wash, how you eat, how you pray and the guards would talk to you perhaps because we sounded more like the guards themselves and western that they did not think that we had those same vulnerabilities. They undoubtedly thought we had vulnerabilities, but different ones such as liking to talk to people, not liking to be alone, etc., and those were the ones they focused on with us.)

According to Bisher they seemed obsessed with what he was doing in Gambia and who sent him there and where he got the money from to go and to finance their business project. They were still asking him about a battery charger that he had in his possession in his baggage on the plane. The Americans were asking him about that.'

Moazzam Begg

'Moazzam Begg we never saw. We only heard about him, paticularly from Saad Al Madini, who was a Pakistani brought up in Saudi Arabia. He had been in Bagram Airbase with Moazzam Begg and he had himself been taken from Bagram Airbase. He had been we think handed over by Indonesia to the Americans, kept in Bagram Airbase, taken from Bagram Airbase to Egypt where he had been tortured and then taken back to Bagram and then to Guantanamo.

While we never saw Moazzam Begg, we did talk to guards who had had contact with him and they told us that he had been in isolation all the time he was there and had only seen them and no one else. Four guards told us that he was in a very bad way. In addition, he was in Bagram for a year and no one that we know of had ever been there for a year and must be in a worse state coming out of it. People coming from there used to tell us that there was a British guy imprisoned there and that must have been Moazzam Begg.

We don't know but have the impression that he may have had 'admissions' forced out of him at Bagram which he did not want to continue when he got to Guantanamo Bay and the authorities kept him in isolation to stop him being able to go back on what he may have said or to have the chance of getting any support from anyone else that might cause him to resist what they wanted. We believe that he was in isolation in Camp Delta and then in isolation in Camp Echo. The impression we have is that the point of keeping people in complete isolation in Camp Echo was so that they would in every way be under the control of the people who held them there. They would have no other information than what they were given by the guards or the interrogators and would be obliged to put all their trust in what they said and would know nothing whatsoever about what was happening in the outside world or even in Guantanamo Bay. The guards were especially picked to go to Echo. We talked to people who had come back from Camp Echo.'

Mamdouh Habib

'One was Mamdouh Habib, who was the Australian. He said that there was no natural light at all there. Even when you went to the shower, which was 'outside', it was still sealed off so you couldn't see any natural light at all. You couldn't tell what time of day or night it was. You were in a room and a guard was sitting outside watching you 24 hours a day. That was his job, just to sit outside the cell and watch you.

Habib himself was in catastrophic shape, mental and physical. As a result of his having been tortured in Egypt where he was taken from Bagram and then brought back, he used to bleed from his nose, mouth and ears when he was asleep. We would say he was about 40 years of age. He got no medical attention for this. We used to hear him ask but his interrogator said that he shouldn't have any. The medics would come and see him and then after he'd asked for medical help they would come back and say if you cooperate with your interrogators then we can do something. (Shafiq says 'Habib told me this and I have also heard them say it to other detainees as well'.) Asif recollects that 'another man who'd been taken to Egypt and tortured there, Saad Al Madini, was also refused medical assistance for the same reason. We know from Al Madini that he had had electrodes put on his knees and something had happened to his bladder and he had problems going to the toilet. He told us that when he was in interrogation he was told by the interrogators that if he cooperated he would be first in line for medical treatment.'

Omar Khadr

Rhuhel recollects 'the same thing also, we are aware, happened to a young Canadian man, Omar Khadr, who was aged 17 when we left. He had been shot three times at point blank range and his lung punctured and had shrapnel in one eye and a cataract in the other. They would not operate on him. He was told that was because he would not cooperate. We were told one time when he was in isolation he was on the floor very badly ill. The guards called the medics and they said they couldn't see him because the interrogators had refused to let them. We don't know what happened to him (he had had come sort of operation when he was still in Afghanistan but he was in constant pain in Guantanamo and still undoubtedly is and they would not give him pain killers.' (He was one door from Rhuhel in the same block and all three used to talk to him).

Mohamed Rajab

'One man, a Yemeni, Mohamed Rajab, was in a particularly bad state. Every two hours he would get moved from cell to cell, 24 hours a day, seven days a week, sometimes cell to cell, sometimes block to block, over a period of eight months. He was deprived of sleep because of this and he was also deprived of medical attention. He'd lost a lot of weight. We were aware that he had a painful medical problem, haemorrhoids, and that treatment was refused unless he cooperated . He said he would cooperate and had an operation. However, the operation was not performed correctly and he still had problems. He would not cooperate. We were aware that shortly before we came back to England he was put into Romeo block where you were stripped naked. We would see people go and come for Romeo. When they went they would go fully clothed. When they came back they would only have shorts on. They told us that they would have all their clothes taken off in the cell. The Red Cross is aware of this. If the interrogators after that thought you should be allowed clothes, then you were allowed them. This appeared to be an open-ended process depending on the interrogation and the interrogators. The people we know who went to that block were not people who caused problems or were disruptive. The whole application of these measures was entirely to do with interrogators and whether they thought they were getting out of them what they could and should get out of them. All the Bosnians were there for instance.'

Algerian detainees kidnapped in Bosnia

'By Bosnians we mean six Algerians who were unlawfully taken from Bosnia to Guantanamo Bay. They told us how they had won their Court case in Bosnia. As they walked out of Court, Americans were there and grabbed them and took them to Camp X-Ray, January 20, 2002. They arrived five days after us. They were kept naked in their cells. They were taken to interrogation for hours on end. They were short shackled for sometimes days on end. They were deprived of their sleep. They never got letters, nor books, nor reading materials. The Bosnians had the same interrogators for a while as we did and so we knew the names which were the same as ours and they were given a very hard time by those. They told us that the interrogators said if they didn't cooperate that they could ensure that something would happen to their families in Algeria and in Bosnia. They had dual nationality. They had families in Bosnia as well as in Algeria.

(From what we could see interrogators used to prey on particular groups of nationality so that Europeans would have the same interrogators, North Africans would have the same, etc.). One of the methods of interrogation was to say that someone in Cuba had told them that we were in a particular place, for instance, the video we've described and training camps in Kandahar. When we asked who it was, they would not tell us.'

(On one occasion Asif was told who had implicated him because he was shown the photograph of a particular detainee in Guantanamo and told that that man had implicated him and said that you were in a mosque in a training camp in Afghanistan. However, this was a detainee whom Asif knew was mentally ill. Before Asif was told this the man was placed in a cell opposite him for about five days and then taken away and it was after that that Asif was accused. 'We could see the process by which the interrogators seemed to get excited, because they finally got some piece of "real" evidence and simply didn't care that it had come from someone who was mentally unbalanced. One of the interrogators did also let slip that another detainee had identified us as the three who were in the video and said he'd seen us in Guantanamo Bay.' (Shafiq recollects examples of interrogators inventing 'information' about us, about the three, and then informing other detainees of it. For example, one detainee came back after interrogation and said he'd been told that Shafiq said that he and another detainee should not be put together because they were in dispute with each other which was completely untrue. Shafiq had never said anything like that.

'We were told by one Algerian (not one of the Bosnian Algerians) that he had been taken to interrogation and been forced to stand naked. He also told us he had been forced to watch a video supposedly showing two detainees dressed in orange, one sodomising the other and was told that it would happen to him if he didn't cooperate.'

An issue that all three men have concerns about is the treatment of those detainees from countries with a worse human rights record than the UK. Whilst in the Chinese block Asif managed to understand from one of the other detainees that they had originally all denied they were from China. They had apparently said they were Afghani. He says that they were very rarely interviewed. Eventually the Americans told them that if they admitted where they were from they would not tell their governments (it seems they did not know if they were Chinese or from one of the Southern republics due to their dialect). The detainees admitted to being Chinese and within one month Chinese officials arrived to interrogate them. The Chinese officials told them that the US had provided full co-operation. If they are returned to China they will all be executed. All three men report similar concerns in relation to the Russian detainees. It seems that a number of these (possibly 20) have been returned to Russia and their fate is unknown.

David Hicks

Asif says 'I first saw David Hicks in Camp X-Ray. He was a very surprising sight. A tiny white guy not more than 5'3" with a lot of tattoos on him. He told us he had endured an extremely bad experience having been held on a ship where he had been interrogated by Americans and hooded and beaten. Despite that experience, he was in better shape then than he was when we last saw him in Mike block. We thought that he had gone downhill. By downhill we mean that he seemed to be losing all hope and more willing to cooperate as a result. We were interrogated a lot but he used to get interrogated every two to three days, sometimes every day. He was told that if he didn't cooperate he would never go home. It started when he was moved to Delta, that he began to be moved all the time. They wouldn't let him settle with anyone. We met him again in Mike block after Delta and had the impression that he was being forced to make admissions, the "force" consisting of offers of benefits if he cooperated and removal of anything that could make life slightly easier if he did not. We were aware for instance that he needed essential medical treatment for a hernia and that he was told he would only get it if he cooperated. We do not know the reason for his appearance when he arrived at Mike block; he had always been proud of his hair, but when he arrived there his head hair was shaved off, although he still had a beard. We were told by some guards that he was taken to Echo after he started cooperating and that in Echo he had access to more basic comforts as a reward, although it is our understanding that he was in Camp Echo i.e. in complete isolation from the summer of 2003 onwards and we presume still there, where the only people he could communicate with would be interrogators. The same guards also told us that he had been taken out of Echo for another operation, but we don't know if that is correct.'

The Kuwaitis

'Fouad Mahmoud Al Rabiah was a businessman, we understand, who had studied in America and graduated from Miami in aeronautical engineering. To us he sounded Scottish. He had lived in England/Scotland for approximately ten years. He was given a particularly hard time, being constantly moved around, every two hours, after General Miller came to the Camp. He took his polygraph test and passed a long time ago and was initially sent to the best section of the Camp but then brought back again after a while. He got extremely harsh treatment including short shackling. Because he was educated, we understand, wealthy, and they were determined that he had to be part of a cell. We understood that he was seized in Pakistan, basically sold by the Pakistanis and then the Americans invented accusations to try and fit. In 2004 the Kuwaiti government came and told all the Kuwaitis that they would be going home in June. When they wanted to know what would happen to them when they got home, they were told "you will find out when you get home." We could see that he was suffering from serious depression, losing weight in a substantial way and very stressed because of the constant moves, deprived of sleep and seriously worried about the consequences for his children. Every father in the camp had a huge worry about his family which added to the stress.' Shafiq recollects when he was next to him in isolation that he was suffering from serious stomach pains and that medication was denied. He was told that he couldn't receive medication unless he cooperated.

Other detainees (including detainees sold to the Americans)

Asif describes a disturbing number of detainees who have clearly been sold. All three are convinced that there must be a paper trail which will show huge sums of money paid out by the USA for many of those now in Guantanamo. These are some examples (some of the names are familial names, as is customary).

a) 'Two brothers from Pakistan, one is a scholar the other a reporter, reason they are there because they were having a feud with another family, the other family told some people they are al Qaeda now they are in Cuba. Both were sure that the Americans were paying money for captives.

b) Numerous other people in Cuba who are from Afghanistan and Pakistan were sure they had been sold by corrupt individuals. A lot of people who were having land disputes were sold by the disputers to the Americans. These people were brought to Cuba. The Americans know they are innocent but still they are not letting them go.

c) Abu Ahmed Makki, a Saudi Arabian citizen married to a Pakistani wife lived in Pakistan with his wife and was arrested in Pakistan by the Pakistan authorities. Most of his possessions were taken including his motorbike and cash. Upon his release in Pakistan by the authorities he asked for his valuables back but he was re-arrested and handed over to the Americans who took him to Cuba and he has been there for over two years. He was told he should not be there but they wanted him to spy in the camp for them. He was told once he had cooperated and helped the Americans they would release him.

d) Abu Ahmad Sudani, a teacher in Pakistan who has a wife and a child in Pakistan believes he also was sold to the American forces. He was told that he would be released over a year ago but he is still in Cuba. He doesn't know when they will release him. He wants to go to Pakistan because his wife and child are in Pakistan. His wife and child are Pakistani nationality and he is a Sudani.'

e) One Afghani man, a farmer about 55 years old, is a farmer from Bamyam. He was next to Shafiq. He speaks Farsi and although in Cuba for over a year was only interrogated on two occasions; on one occasion there was no Farsi translator and he was brought back to his cage. He does not know what he has done to be in Cuba. He doesn't even know where Cuba is! He is depressed, scared and badly affected.

Camp Four

Asif says 'numerous other detainees have been told that their interrogation has finished, they have passed numerous tests e.g. lie detector, stress analyser test. They have been taken to Camp 4 but they still have not been released.

It is called a medium security section. When we were in Guantanamo there were four blocks. One block has four bays in it. Each bay has ten or twelve people in. Instead of wearing orange they all would be wearing white. These are detainees who are always shown on TV playing football. They don't wear chains or shackles. They are said to be people who are about to go home but they yet have been there about one year. These are examples of the hundreds of people who should never have been in Cuba in the first place. The authorities seem paralysed. They can't send them home, they don't bother to interrogate them so they are just stuck.'

HEALTH AND HUMAN RIGHTS

In its editorial of 21 August 2004, the medical journal The Lancet *responded to some of the issues about the treatment of detainees at Guantanamo raised in the Statement of Shafiq Rasul, Asif Iqbal and Rhuhel Ahmed, and asked 'How complicit are doctors in abuses of detainees?' This editorial is reprinted below. The article by Steven Miles, on 'Abu Ghraib: its legacy for military medicine', which it mentions, is available on the web (www.thelancet.com).*

Almost 3 years ago, we asked, 'Does the western world still take human rights seriously?' We did so in response to the UK's 2001 Anti-terrorism, Crime, and Security Act, which itself was a reaction to the events of September 11 that year. We were disturbed by a *Newsweek* columnist's suggestion that the use of torture on suspected terrorists should be considered as a legitimate means of obtaining information. As more details about the treatment of detainees in the Abu Ghraib prison in Iraq and the US Guantanamo Bay detention centre in Cuba come to light, disquiet about contemplating or debating the use of torture to secure information has given way to certainty that this is precisely what took place under US command. The answer to our question posed three years ago is clearly 'no'; human rights have become a casualty in the desperate attempt to get results in the war against terrorism. The question we now need to ask is, what part have doctors played in these abuses?

The UK Court of Appeal ruled last week in a two-to-one judgment that evidence obtained by torture is admissible as long as it is not procured by British officials. The ruling was made in response to an appeal brought by ten foreign nationals detained in the UK for more than two years without charge or trial under the Anti-terrorism, Crime and Security Act. The dissenting judge, Lord Justice Neumeister, argued that 'by using torture or even by adopting the fruits of torture, a democratic state is weakening its case against terrorists, by adopting their methods, thereby losing the moral high ground an open democratic society enjoys'. The case will almost certainly go on to the House of Lords.

Currently, 585 people are held in Guantanamo Bay without charge and many have been there for two years or longer. 156 have so far been released. The official number of suicide attempts is given as 34. None has been successful because detainees are checked by guards every 45 seconds. According to the Guantanamo Bay press officer, about 10% are receiving counselling or medical treatment for mental illness. However the number of detainees with mental health problems may be much higher, given the details of detention conditions and methods of interrogations that are coming to light through the reports of those released. Lawyers for three UK citizens arrested in Afghanistan and held in Guantanamo Bay, who were sent back to the UK in March this year only to be released without charges by UK authorities, have compiled a report based on interviews with their clients. This report describes how confessions that were later proven by MI5 to be false were made allegedly under coercive conditions. How can the UK Home Secretary David Blunkett and the Court of Appeal justify using, for example, such evidence to detain people indefinitely?

Even more disturbing is the emerging evidence that doctors and other medical personnel have helped, covered up, or stood by silently when humiliation, degrading treatment, and physical abuses have taken place. As Steven Miles describes in this week's issue of *The Lancet*, there are now reports of medical personnel in Afghanistan and Iraq allegedly abusing detainees, falsifying and delaying death certificates, and covering up homicides. No unprompted reports of abuses were initiated by medical personnel before the official investigation into practices at Abu Ghraib. At Guantanamo Bay, medical records were routinely shared with interrogators in a clear breach of confidentiality and with the knowledge that such information can be misused despite objections by the medical team of the International Committee of the Red Cross, who in protest suspended their medical visits.

Military doctors can be placed in a difficult position, but the problem of dual loyalty, to patients and to their employers, is well recognised. Guidelines and codes of practice state that doctors, even in military forces, must first and foremost be concerned about their patients and bound by principles of medical ethics. Given these events, the World Medical Association saw the need to re-emphasise its strong and unambiguous 1975 Tokyo Declaration in June: 'Doctors shall not countenance, condone, or participate in torture or other forms of degrading procedures…in all situations, including armed conflict and civil strife'. As one of the other few medical bodies to speak out, members of Physicians for Human Rights wrote an open letter on August 6 to James Schlesinger, Chair of the independent panel to review US Department of Defense detention operations (and due to report later this month), questioning the role and use of physicians and other medical personnel in detention centres in Afghanistan, Iraq, and Guantanamo Bay.

Health-care workers should now break their silence. Those who were involved in or witnessed ill-treatment need to give a full and accurate account of events at Abu Ghraib and Guantanamo Bay. Those who are still in positions where dual commitments prevent them from putting the rights of their patients above other interests, should protest loudly and refuse cooperation with authorities. The wider non-military medical community should unite in support of their colleagues and condemn torture and inhumane and degrading practices against detainees. Abu Ghraib should serve as an eleventh hour wake-up call for the western world to rediscover and live by the values enshrined in its international treaties and democratic constitutions. ©*The Lancet*

BOSTON SOCIAL FORUM

The Boston Social Forum met in July. Tony Simpson sent this report from New England.

The keepers of the Peace Vigil gather every Thursday tea-time in Depot Square in the small town of Lexington, a dozen miles north of Boston. 'End the Occupation – Bring the Troops Home Now' is inscribed on one banner; 'The US used to be against Tyranny' on another. The banners are held up by a small group of residents who exchange greetings with the passers-by. Drive-time commuters on nearby Massachusetts Avenue honk their support.

'There is overwhelming sympathy for our position,' says a local Democratic Party activist and vigil organiser. This is especially significant as we are on the eve of the Democratic National Convention, or 'DNC', at the Fleet Center in Boston. Kerry/Edwards bumper stickers sprout along Mass Ave.

Whether or not to vote for Kerry was the subject of long debates across town, at the University of Massachusetts, or UMASS, where the Boston Social Forum met on the weekend prior to the Convention. The prevailing view appeared to be that getting rid of Bush was the first priority. 'Then the work really starts, on November 3rd', as Lesley Cagan, the canny organiser of United for Justice and Peace, put it. UJP want to fill the streets of New York with protesters on 29th August, the eve of the Republican National Convention. That will pose some interesting questions for the authorities.

In Boston, UJP and others refused to comply with the 'Free Speech Zone' established by the city authorities near to the Fleet Center. This walled cage, allegedly for up to 4,000 people playing 'sardines', was the subject of a legal challenge by the American Civil Liberties Union. The judge found that the cage was certainly inimical to free speech, but nevertheless upheld that it was necessary to put people in it if they wished to register a protest during the Convention. In response, the UCJ and others refused to be complicit in their own muzzling and caging.

Not surprisingly, Palestinian groups protesting against Israel's Wall and land-grab, did decide that the walled cage was a fitting venue and symbol for their own protests. Otherwise, as long-time South African activist Dennis Brutus told the Forum, let's declare 'Free-Speech Zones' all round the city. 'After all, isn't all the US supposed to be a free-speech zone?'

'It's never been easier to talk to people about the war', according to Jim

Caplan of the Somerville Teachers' Association, during a workshop on 'Organised Labour Against the War', which receives much of its funding from the US public services union, SEIU. 'More and more people are against it.' Tony Donaghy, President of the RMT, spoke of a similar situation in Britain and Ireland. Mention of Tony Blair elicited loud hisses from Forum audiences

The 'Peace Track' within the Forum was organised by the American Friends Service Committee, a Quaker organisation. The impetus for this came initially from Ken Coates and the European Network for Peace and Human Rights (ENPHR), whose meetings in the European Parliament in Brussels were initiated by the Russell Foundation. The European Network had long wanted to strengthen its contacts and establish a dialogue with peace movement organisations in the United States. AFSC picked up the ball and ran with it at the Forum, broadening the participation to include activists from Asia, Africa and Europe, as well as from the United States, under the rubric of 'A World Working Together for Peace'.

War and peace will certainly be amongst the issues to the fore when the European Social Forum comes to London, from 14 to 17 October. Thousands are expected to participate. 'We are many, they are few', as Rae Street of CND reminded the closing session of the Boston Social Forum.

Meanwhile, back in Lexington, where, in 1775, the shot that echoed round the world marked the beginning of the removal of the British from their American colonies, *Fahrenheit 9/11* continues to play to packed houses at the Lexington Flick, just across the street from Depot Square. The US peace movement is becoming altogether harder to ignore.

WORLD TRIBUNAL ON IRAQ

Ayse Berktay in Turkey has sent this note about the work of the World Tribunal on Iraq.

The World Tribunal on Iraq (WTI) is a worldwide initiative born out of the global outcry against the war in Iraq. Taking its cue from the Russell Tribunal of the late 1960s, it is aimed at challenging the silences of our time around the aggression against Iraq and seeking the truth about the war and occupation in Iraq. This will be a record of wrongs, violations and crimes as well as suffering, resistance and silenced voices. This will be a solemn process of listening, reflection, evaluation and informed judgement based on concrete evidence. This will be a call to conscience and a call to act to preserve our futures.

The World Tribunal on Iraq comprises various sessions around the world, each focusing on different aspects of the aggression against Iraq, culminating in Istanbul on 20 March 2005. What is unique and exciting about the Tribunal is that it is a truly global network of local peoples' initiatives, who are determined to bring out and record the truth, to elaborate on its implications for our struggles, for humanity and for the world at large. We are aware that in this process there may arise issues that need further investigation, deliberation and work, that may not be finalised within the scope of the Tribunal. We hope to be able to indicate at least such need and call on new initiatives to follow these up. We believe our power of enforcement lies in our ability, as global movements, to appeal to public conscience and to mobilise around the truths brought out, to create political pressure. This is how we hope to contribute to the worldwide struggle for peace, truth and justice.

* * *

A Session of the World Tribunal on Iraq devoted to 'Media Wrongs Against Truth and Humanity' will take place in Rome from 10 to 13 February, 2005. The following statement about the Session is being circulated for endorsement and support by WTI-Italy and the Peoples' Law Programme of the Lelio Basso International Foundation.

The World Tribunal on Iraq is an international citizens' initiative to examine and establish the truth in relation to the war and occupation of Iraq, in order that it may contribute to the empowerment of civil society movements for peace, human rights and justice. It is comprised of various Sessions held around the world (Sessions already held include Brussels, New York, Hiroshima-Tokyo, and Copenhagen) culminating in a Final Session in Istanbul in March 2005. This is a call to individuals, social movements, associations and organisations to endorse the Rome Session of the World Tribunal on Iraq on 'Media Wrongs Against Truth and Humanity'.

The session in Rome focuses specifically on the role and responsibilities of the 'media' with respect to 'truth-telling'. The context of the war and subsequent developments in Iraq raise many issues of public concern about media disinformation and 'propaganda'. However, little of the discussion thus far has involved recognition of the peoples who have been wronged! The aim of the session is to return the focus to the media's responsibilities to the social context of human lives, and to provide an empowered peoples' language to demand accountability.

In contrast to notions of 'professional inadequacy' that have dominated most considerations of the media's role in relation to the war in Iraq, the Session will examine the issues from the point of view of 'wrongs' committed against three constituencies of the affected: the peoples of Iraq; the citizens of the 'Coalition'; and 'Humanity' – the global human population in general, with particular emphasis on the South. The Session will consider the following charges:

1. Wrongs committed against the Peoples of Iraq:
- A Wrong of Aggression – complicity in the waging of an aggressive war and perpetuating a regime of occupation that is widely regarded as guilty of war crimes and crimes against humanity.
- A Wrong of Silence – neglect of the duty to give privilege and dignity to voices of suffering.

2. Wrongs committed against the Peoples of the 'Coalition': (in addition to the above)
- A Wrong of Deception – complicity, through the validation and dissemination of disinformation, in enabling the fraudulent misappropriation of human and financial resources for war, and away from social development.
- A Wrong of Incitement – culpability for inciting an ideological climate of fear, racism, xenophobia and violence.

3. Wrongs committted against Humanity: (in addition to the above)
- A Wrong of Exclusion – complicity in the exclusion of the voices and visions of the social majorities for people's security and well-being by privileging instead the priorities of the minority corporate-military elite.
- A Wrong of Usurpation – complicity in enabling the usurpation of human aspirations – for peace and justice – for political and economic profit.

Underpinning the motivation of the World Tribunal on Iraq in general, and the Rome Session in particular, is the conviction that people as concerned social actors retain the right and the duty to establish the truths upon which social judgement on matters relating to peace, justice and human wellbeing may be reached, and to demand that the institutions of power so act. The unprecedented peoples' uprisings against the violations committed in the name of 'liberation' and 'global security' against the peoples of Iraq have demonstrated that the deceptions of power no longer hold sway with much of the global population; that we, as peoples of the world, must act to reclaim for humanity the values of solidarity and justice is clear. The beginning of a Peoples' Law movement is upon us. The Rome Session of the World Tribunal on Iraq is intended as a contribution towards this movement.

We hope that you will be with us in this endeavour. We seek your endorsement and support for Truth, Peace and Justice.

For further information, or if you would like to provide additional support, please contact the following at WTI Italy: Jayan Nayar – Walter Musco, Peoples' Law Programme, Lelio Basso International Foundation, Via della Dogana Vecchia, 5 – 00186 Rome Italy, Tel. 0039.06.68.65.352 – Fax 0039.06.68.77.774, wti-italia@libero.it

INTERNATIONAL COURT FINDS ISRAEL'S WALL 'ILLEGAL'

These are some excerpts of the Advisory Opinion that the International Court of Justice in The Hague has rendered in the case concerning the Legal Consequences of the Construction of a Wall in the Occupied Palestinian Territory. The Opinion was requested by the UN General Assembly, and is dated 9 July 2004.

The construction of the wall being built by Israel, the occupying Power, in the

Occupied Palestinian Territory, including in and around East Jerusalem, and its associated regime, are contrary to international law.

Israel is under an obligation to terminate its breaches of international law; it is under an obligation to cease forthwith the works of construction of the wall being built in the Occupied Palestinian Territory, including in and around East Jerusalem, to dismantle forthwith the structure therein situated, and to repeal or render ineffective forthwith all legislative and regulatory acts relating thereto, in accordance with paragraph 151 of this Opinion.

Israel is under obligation to make reparation for all damage caused by the construction of the wall in the Occupied Palestinian Territory, including in and around East Jerusalem.

All States are under an obligation not to recognise the illegal situation resulting from the construction of the wall, and not to render aid or assistance in maintaining the situation created by such construction; all States, parties to the Fourth Geneva Convention relative to the Protection of Civilian Persons in Time of War of 12 August 1949 have in addition, the obligation, while respecting the United Nations Charter and international law, to ensure compliance by Israel with international humanitarian law as embodied in that Convention.

The United Nations, and especially the General Assembly and the Security Council, should consider what further action is required to bring to an end the illegal situation resulting from the construction of the wall and the associated regime, taking due account of the present Advisory Opinion…

The Court determines the rules and principles of international law which are relevant to the question posed by the General Assembly.

The Court begins by citing, with reference to Article 2, paragraph 4, of the United Nations Charter and to General Assembly resolution 2625 (XXV), the principles of the prohibition of the threat or use of force and the illegality of any territorial acquisition by such means, as reflected in customary international law. It further cites the principle of self-determination of peoples, as enshrined in the Charter and reaffirmed by resolution 2625 (XXV). As regards international humanitarian law, the Court refers to the provisions of the Hague Regulation of 1907, which have become part of customary law, as well as the Fourth Geneva Convention relative to the Protection of Civilian Persons in Time of War of 1949, applicable in those Palestinian territories which before the armed conflict of 1967 lay to the east of the 1949 Armistice demarcation line (or 'Green Line') and were occupied by Israel during that conflict. The Court further notes that certain human rights instruments (International Covenant on Civil and Political Rights, International Covenant on Economic, Social and Cultural Rights and the United Nations Convention on the Rights of the Child) are applicable in the Occupied Palestinian Territory.

The Court considers the information furnished to it regarding the impact of the construction of the wall on the daily life of the inhabitants of the Occupied Palestinian Territory (destruction or requisition of private property, restrictions on freedom of movement, confiscation of agricultural land, cutting off of access to primary water sources, etc); finds that the construction of the wall and its associated regime are contrary to the revised provisions of the Hague Regulations of 1947 and of the Fourth Geneva Convention; that they impede the liberty of movement of the inhabitants of the territory as guaranteed by the International Covenant on Civil and Political Rights; and that they also impede the exercise by the persons concerned of the right to work, to health, to education and to an adequate standard of living as proclaimed in the International Covenant on Economic, Social and Cultural Rights, and in the Convention on the Rights of the Child. Lastly, the Court finds that this construction and its associated regime, coupled with the establishment of settlements, are tending to alter the demographic composition of the Occupied Palestinian Territory and thereby contravene the Fourth Geneva Convention and the relevant Security Council resolutions.

In conclusion, the Court considers that Israel cannot rely on a right of self-defence or on a state of necessity in order to preclude the wrongfulness of the construction of the wall. The Court accordingly finds that the construction of the wall and its associated regime are contrary to international law.

RUSSELL ON RADIO WINS AWARD

Russell's warning of man's peril from the hydrogen bomb, delivered in 1954, electrifies Michele Ernsting's award-winning radio history of the construction of the first nuclear and hydrogen bombs, and the emergence of the anti-nuclear movement in their aftermath. Everyone interested in the nuclear era will want to hear 'WMD', which is radio broadcasting at its best. Certainly, that was the view of judges in the international affairs section of the 2004 New York Festivals, which recognises 'the world's best work' in radio programming and promotion. Radio Netherlands, the Dutch foreign service, won a gold medal for *Weapons of Mass Destruction: The Race,* which can be heard via their web site, given below. (http://www.rnw.nl/special/en/html/030423wmd2.html)

AFGHANISTAN: THE SUBVERSION OF RELIEF

In late July 2004, *Médecins sans Frontières* (MSF) pulled out of Afghanistan after having provided humanitarian assistance there for nearly 24 years. The reasons for the organisation's withdrawal included a deterioration of the security environment in Afghanistan and, more importantly, the misuse of humanitarian aid by US military forces in the country.

Médecins sans Frontières also said it was unhappy with the lack of progress in a government investigation of the killing of five of its aid workers in the northern province of Baghdis in June, presumably by insurgents. MSF, which employed about 1,400 local staff and 80 international staff, ended all its operations last week.

'In Afghanistan, the US-backed coalition has constantly sought to use and co-opt humanitarian assistance to build support for its military and political ambitions,' says Michael Neuman, programme officer at *Médecins sans Frontières*.

'By doing so, providing aid is no longer perceived as being a neutral and impartial act, and this is endangering humanitarian aid workers and this is jeopardising assistance to the Afghan people – the assistance which is needed'.

Neuman said *Médecins sans Frontières* has been raising general concerns about the blurring of humanitarian and military objectives for years. 'We have done this at meetings with officials for different countries, including the United States and the United Kingdom,' he added. Wherever there are coalition forces – or even United Nations agencies – mixing political and humanitarian mandates, 'you will continue to see a danger for impartial, neutral and humanitarian action,' he said.

'Humanitarian assistance is only possible when armed actors respect the safety of humanitarian actors. This is why we are calling on the coalition to cease all activity which tries to put humanitarian aid in the service of their political and military objectives,' Neuman added.

'We understand why MSF feels that their position has become untenable. Oxfam International is gravely concerned about the deteriorating security situation in Afghanistan, which is increasingly affecting the ability for humanitarian and development organisations to work,' said Caroline Green of Oxfam. In 2004, six staff members from Oxfam partner organisations have been killed in attacks in provinces previously considered to be relatively safe. 'However, we feel strongly that Oxfam is providing important services to the poor people of Afghanistan and the risks we face are currently manageable and we feel that we are able to continue working in Afghanistan,' continued Green.

HIROSHIMA'S PEACE DECLARATION

Tadatoshi Akiba, the Mayor of Hiroshima, made this declaration on 6 August 2004, the fifty-ninth anniversary of the atomic bombing of his city.

'Nothing will grow for 75 years.' Fifty-nine years have passed since the August sixth when Hiroshima was so thoroughly obliterated that many succumbed to such doom. Dozens of corpses still bearing the agony of that day, souls torn abruptly from their loved ones and their hopes for the future, have recently re-surfaced on Ninoshima Island, warning us to beware the utter inhumanity of the atomic bombing and the gruesome horror of war.

Unfortunately, the human race still lacks both a lexicon capable of fully expressing that disaster, and sufficient imagination to fill the gap. Thus, most of us float idly in the current of the day, clouding with self-indulgence the lens of reason through which we should be studying the future, and blithely turning our backs on the courageous few.

As a result, the egocentric worldview of the US government reaches extremes. Ignoring the United Nations and its foundation of international law, the United States has resumed research on making nuclear weapons smaller and more 'usable.' Elsewhere, the chains of violence and retaliation know no end: reliance on violence-amplifying terror, and North Korea, among others, buying into the worthless policy of 'nuclear insurance', are salient symbols of our times.

We must perceive and tackle this human crisis within the context of human history. In the year leading up to the 60th anniversary, which begins a new cycle of rhythms in the interwoven fabric that binds humankind and nature, we must return to our point of departure, the unprecedented A-bomb experience. In the coming year, we must sow the seeds of new hope and cultivate a strong future-oriented movement.

To that end, the city of Hiroshima, along with the Mayors for Peace and our 611 member cities in 109 countries and regions, hereby declare the period beginning today and lasting until August 9, 2005, to be a Year of Remembrance and Action for a Nuclear-Free World. Our goal is to bring forth a beautiful 'flower' for the 75th anniversary of the atomic bombings, namely, the total elimination of all nuclear weapons from the face of the Earth by the year 2020. Only then will we have truly resurrected hope for life on this 'nothing will grow' planet.

The seeds we sow today will sprout in May 2005. At the Review Conference for the Treaty on the Non-Proliferation of Nuclear Weapons (NPT) to be held in New York, the Emergency Campaign to Ban Nuclear Weapons will bring together cities, citizens, and non-governmental organisations from around the world to work with like-minded nations towards the adoption of an action programme that incorporates, as an interim goal, the signing in 2010 of a Nuclear Weapons Convention to serve as the framework for eliminating nuclear weapons by 2020.

Around the world, this Emergency Campaign is generating waves of support. This past February, the European Parliament passed by overwhelming majority a resolution specifically supporting the Mayors for Peace campaign. At its general assembly in June, the United States Conference of Mayors, representing 1183 US cities, passed by acclamation an even stronger resolution.

We anticipate that Americans, a people of conscience, will follow the lead of their mayors and form the mainstream of support for the Emergency Campaign as an expression of their love for humanity and desire to discharge their duty, as the lone superpower, to eliminate nuclear weapons.

We are striving to communicate the message of the *hibakusha* around the world and promote the Hiroshima-Nagasaki Peace Study Course to ensure, especially, that future generations will understand the inhumanity of nuclear weapons and the cruelty of war. In addition, during the coming year, we will implement a project that will mobilise adults to read eyewitness accounts of the atomic bombings to children everywhere.

The Japanese government, as our representative, should defend the Peace Constitution, of which all Japanese should be proud, and work diligently to rectify the trend toward open acceptance of war and nuclear weapons increasingly prevalent at home and abroad. We demand that our government act on its obligation as the only A-bombed nation and become the world leader for nuclear weapons abolition, generating an anti-nuclear tsunami by fully and enthusiastically supporting the Emergency Campaign led by the Mayors for Peace. We further demand more generous relief measures to meet the needs of our ageing *hibakusha*, including those living overseas and those exposed in black rain areas.

Rekindling the memory of Hiroshima and Nagasaki, we pledge to do everything in our power during the coming year to ensure that the 60th anniversary of the atomic bombings will see a budding of hope for the total abolition of nuclear weapons. We humbly offer this pledge for the peaceful repose of all atomic bomb victims.

THIS SEPTEMBER...
GIVE PEACE A CHANCE

THE BEAUTY QUEEN'S GUIDE TO WORLD PEACE
MONEY, POWER AND MAYHEM IN THE TWENTY-FIRST CENTURY
BY DAN PLESCH

" A unique book which embraces all the issues of central importance to the future of humankind. This is a must read to all seeking a peaceful world order in the twenty-first century. "
PROFESSOR JOSEPH ROTBLAT,
Nobel Peace Prize laureate

In this groundbreaking and controversial new book writer, broadcaster and activist Dan Plesch offers every beauty queen what they really want: **WORLD PEACE**

Arguing that there can be no military solution to terrorism, he uses a wealth of historical evidence and an unrivalled command of the facts about military conflict in the twenty-first century to make a powerful case against the warmongers and provide a compelling blueprint for peace.

September 2004 • £8.99 • Politico's Publishing
020 7798 1610

Reviews

Finding square circles in Iraq

Hans Blix, *Disarming Iraq: The Search for Weapons of Mass Destruction*, Bloomsbury, 285 pages, ISBN 0747573549, £16.99
John Prados, *Hoodwinked: The documents that reveal how Bush sold us a war*, New Press, 375 pages, ISBN 1565849027, $19.95

There can be few public servants more diligent and persistent than Hans Blix, and few who are more implacably devoted to pursuing their allotted tasks. Enormous pressures were generated by the belligerent powers, with the intention of influencing Blix' findings: it was presumed that Iraq was stiff with weapons of mass destruction, and that all denials of the innumerable allegations about them were simply lies.

Today, this all seems an age ago. Now, nobody believes in the missing arsenal of Saddam Hussein, with the possible exception of the British Prime Minister, who is deeply entrenched in his own fantasy world, where he relives a happy childhood absconding to the Americas and following football folklore in his imagination.

American mobile exploration teams and site survey teams stomped all over Iraq after Hans Blix' UN weapons' inspectors were excluded from that country, and poked into every corner which had been designated by 'intelligence' as key WMD facilities. Bursting into the Iraqi Special Security Organisation, thought to be the agency responsible for Iraq's effort to hide its weapons programmes, one team smashed into a building, and then, through the dark, came upon another locked door. As they breathlessly forced their entry, they were surprised to find a room entirely full of vacuum cleaners. Team 3, headed by Major Kenneth Deal, noisily found a 'smoking gun' when it visited the Ba'ath Party headquarters. After this discovery, a reporter noted: 'Smoking gun is now a term of dark irony here'. The secret documents which were uncovered turned out to be an Arabic version of A. J. P. Taylor's well-known history of *The Struggle for Mastery in Europe*. It may have been useful to Mr. Blair.

Blix was not allowed the time to investigate either Iraqi vacuum cleaners or the selected works of A. J. P. Taylor. His book, which fastidiously records the events in which he was able to take part, and the pressures to which he was subjected, begins by accepting, not without due agnosticism, the possibility that the Iraqi Government might still be dabbling in weapons of mass destruction. From there on, it records a rapid learning curve.

Of course, during the war with Iran, Western powers, and others, were not interested in promoting United Nations enquiries into nuclear or other weapons in Iraq, because they were fully engaged in the effort to modernise Iraqi arms to overthrow the Ayatollahs. Indeed, from Britain, never averse to military waste, this process was apparently funded by Export Credit Guarantees, at no cost whatever to Saddam's exchequer, but to the detriment of the British taxpayer. No doubt unsavoury revelations about this commerce in WMD would have featured strongly in the Iraqi declaration on its weapons programmes, submitted in response to Resolution 1441 of the Security Council, and subsequently censored so that only permanent members of the Security Council were allowed to read the lion's share of the text, thus avoiding the sniggers of the small fry.

Precisely when did Saddam Hussein determine the destruction of the prohibited weapons which Hans Blix was sent to find?

> 'We now know', says Blix, 'that while the armed operation in Iraq was successful, the main diagnosis suggesting the operation – existence of weapons of mass destruction – appears to have been wrong. It was like surgery intended to remove something malignant finding that the malignancy was not there. Moreover, the absence of prohibited items was most likely a result of the imposition of the regime of inspection, eradication and manufacturing by the UN supported by military pressure from the US and the UK.'

Small wonder that Blix subtitles this part of his narrative 'The mother of all misjudgement'. He asks why it was that Blair and Bush listened so little to the International Atomic Energy Agency, and why Mr. Cheney and Mr. Wolfowitz 'seemed to have had such disdain for the assessments and analyses of the IAEA'.

Blix documents serial shortcomings in the intelligence which sent him on what seems largely to have been a wild goose chase. In fact there was a whole flock of wild geese. John Prados, by contrast, stayed at home and analysed, with great care, the documents which show 'how Bush sold us a war'.

> 'The drum beat of Bush administration published commentary had been uniformly negative. Washington wanted, or at least said it wanted, more inspections, faster inspections, more comprehensive inspections, at a time when the UNMOVIC group in Iraq had only recently arrived, was still getting up to speed, and had just over a week of visits under its belt. The Americans were making all kinds of confident assertions on what Iraq's weapons of mass destruction were. Hans Blix wanted to find them. Blix had received US intelligence briefings before, but all had a general level. He wanted the real skinny-hard data on targets his inspectors could go out and find.'

Resolution 1441 obliged Washington to provide this information, but the Americans were angry when it was requested. Prados remorselessly probes this modesty, reproducing successive documents, and carefully taking them to pieces. He examines, in turn, the Iraqi nuclear programme; unmanned aerial vehicles; allegations about the importation of yellow cake from Niger: and, in depth, the allegations about Saddam's proximity to al Qaeda and responsibility for 9/11.

In truth, it appears from this study that it really makes no difference whether Saddam Hussein did or did not harbour nuclear weapons, or chemical and biological warfare programmes. Neither does it really matter what precise relations Saddam Hussein may have had (or not) with Osama bin Laden. It is quite evident that the American Government itself had closer relations, and bears a heavier weight of responsibility for nurturing bin Laden: but be that as it may, President Bush had resolved upon his war long before the events described in these books took place. These investigations were all part of the choreography, which could not influence the course of events.

It is good to have these detailed accounts from key participants: when will the prehistory of these shocking manoeuvres be fully revealed?

Rosemary Thomas

Raspberry Voluntary

John Kampfner, *Blair's Wars*, The Free Press, 2004, 416 pages, paperback ISBN 0 7432 4830 9, £7.99

The paperback edition of *Blair's Wars*, John Kampfner's aptly titled book, concludes: 'These were not his government's wars, least of all his party's wars. These were Blair's wars.' Kampfner musters a powerful case. Our reviewer of the original hardback edition commented that he 'has written what is perhaps the most important book on the outcome of New Labour, in all the years since 1997'.

For the new edition, Kampfner has added a section entitled 'Damaged Warrior', which includes 'elements of Hutton' (the inquiry into the death of the former weapons' inspector Dr David Kelly), and in which the author 'hopes to have shed new light on the workings of Blair's entourage, from the government's battles with the BBC, to the elusive search for weapons of mass destruction and the tensions this brought to relations with the US, to the legal advice of the Attorney General.'

On Hutton, Kampfner highlights 'the observation by [Jonathan] Powell that the dossier was "a bit of a problem" because it included "nothing to demonstrate a threat, let alone an imminent threat from Saddam' unless Iraq was attacked".' John Morrison, a career intelligence analyst in the Ministry of Defence, put the issue in a sharp perspective when he recently told the BBC's *Panorama* programme that, in response to the Prime Minister's assertion that 'the threat [from Iraq's WMD] is current and serious', that he 'could almost hear the collective raspberry going up round Whitehall'. For his trouble, Mr Morrison was duly sacked from his post as 'investigator' for the Intelligence and Security Committee at Westminster, which oversees Britain's intelligence services. Vindictiveness, it seems, goes together with Blair's innate belligerence.

It is much to be hoped that John Morrison, the valiant Brian Jones, formerly of the Defence Intelligence Staff and author of the memo which provided written testimony of the grave doubts about the claims made for Iraq's chemical weapons capability in Blair's infamous September Dossier, and, indeed, John Kampfner and others will continue to probe and make public the goings-on as Blair railroaded Britain into war on Iraq. Certainly, Lord Butler's report has thrown up many further questions. What, for instance, were Operation Rockingham's actual conclusions in relation to the Iraqi Declaration about its weapons of mass destruction? This was the 12,000 page report that Iraq submitted to the United Nations on 7 December 2002, in accordance with resolution 1441, which Jack Straw subsequently described in *The Times* (5 February 2003) as 'neither full, accurate, nor complete'. What was omitted, if there were no weapons of mass destruction in Iraq? Butler tells us that Operation Rockingham 'acted as the focus for the work tasked by the

Joint Intelligence Committee on the analysis of the declaration' (p.90). (For an extended discussion of the fate of the Iraqi declaration see *Empire No More*! pp187-199 by Ken Coates, Spokesman Books, 2004). And what was Dr Kelly's role in relation to all this? Surely, we haven't yet had the full story.

Kampfner also proves a rich source of New Labour gossip. He chronicles the twists and turns of New Labour's big falling-out with the BBC, over Andrew Gilligan's story about Blair's manipulation of the September dossier, with Peter Mandelson as master of ceremonies:

> 'The polarised views about the Gilligan story were sharpened by the intensity of the personal relationships. By this point Peter Mandelson had re-emerged as a key player at Blair's side. They all went back such a long way – Mandelson had been a lodger at the home of [Gavyn] Davies and his wife, Sue Nye, who runs Gordon Brown's office. [Greg] Dyke and Davies had been prominent Labour supporters. It was Davies and Nye who brought Mandelson and Brown together at their home in 1999 in an attempt to broker a ceasefire. This time, through another BBC-New Labour connection, it was Mandelson's turn to try to fix a deal. Two days before an emergency meeting of the corporation's governors, Mandelson phoned Caroline Thomson, the BBC's head of policy (who is married to Roger Liddle, an ally of Mandelson and long-time aid to Blair on Europe), suggesting a compromise – if the BBC said the story was wrong, the government would say it was a legitimate mistake and that the *Today* programme had been within its rights to broadcast it. Tessa Jowell, the Culture Secretary, urged them to accept the deal. Dyke and Davies pondered it, and rejected it…Over the next few weeks the row not just with [Alastair] Campbell but also with Mandelson intensified. Mandelson suggested to Davies that he was "too weak" to control Dyke. When Davies said it was not a case of weakness, but that he stood by the original story, Mandelson said he was only doing so because he was "a Brownite". He was, Mandelson said, "doing Brown's conspiracies to bring Tony Blair into disrepute…".'

This is a surely a story to which we will have to return. Certainly, the removal of Greg Dyke as Director General of the BBC ushered in the baleful era of Mark Byford, Geoff Hoon's old friend from Leeds University, as stop-gap. BBC Radio News programmes became completely un-listenable, as dumbing down plumbed unfathomable depths. The broadcast world, for a few weeks, was made fit for Mandelson's ear. Meanwhile, Iraq was imploding, although you had to go to Al Jazeera and Robert Fisk in *The Independent* to find out about it.

The autumn promises Greg Dyke's account of these events, which is likely to deliver a fanfare of raspberries. It all helps to bring closer the 'blairectomy'.

Tony Simpson

…Liars can figure

Christina Beatty and Stephen Fothergill, *The Diversion from 'Unemployment' to 'Sickness' across British Regions and Districts,* **Centre for Regional Economic and Social Research, Sheffield Hallam University**

We don't have a problem with unemployment in Britain anymore, do we? According to government ministers supported by most economic pundits and financial journalists the problem is at worst only marginal. Such difficulties that remain can be resolved by better inducements for people to look for work, and heavier penalties for those who fail to do so.

For those who follow what has become the conventional wisdom that there is a suitable job for everybody who wants one, this new study is bound to be an eye-opener. The authors look beyond the comforting statistics of the static or declining monthly claimant count and delve into the reality of hidden unemployment. They arrive at the startling conclusion that more than a million men and women are jobless without being recorded in the official statistics. They conclude that the true figure of unemployment is more than double the official count.

The difficulty in measuring the true extent of those who are out of work lies in changes to the benefit system. Before 1981, the total of those claiming unemployment benefit could be taken as a reasonably accurate measure of those who were out of work. But a series of over 30 changes were introduced by successive Conservative governments, designed to make it more difficult for people to claim benefits, while at the same time helping to disguise the true level of unemployment. Finally, in 1996, the Government substituted Job Seekers' Allowance for Unemployment Benefit. JSA is payable only to those who are deemed to be available and actively looking for work.

When New Labour came into power, in 1997, it did nothing to reverse these changes, but rather sought to tighten the application of restrictions on eligibility for benefit.

The removal of the payment of benefit by right to unemployed people has meant that anyone with a working spouse or a pension from a previous job is debarred or deterred from making a claim: they have to look elsewhere for help. In the absence of alternative work there was another possibility for those suffering from some illness or disability: they could apply for Incapacity Benefit which was not subject to the same restrictions as Job Seekers' Allowance.

Beatty and Fothergill identify what they describe as a 'truly astounding' rise in the numbers claiming Incapacity Benefit over two decades. In 1981, there were 570,000 drawing Invalidity Benefit, as it was then known. By 2003, those on Incapacity Benefit and Severe Disablement Allowance, the successors to the original benefit, had risen incredibly to 2.7 million people! Our two researchers argue convincingly that such a huge increase can hardly be attributed to a general deterioration in the health of the British workforce.

Building on previous studies of their own and of other researchers into the labour market in the coalfields and elsewhere, Beatty and Fothergill are able to demonstrate that large-scale closures and the shrinkage of local employment opportunities do not necessarily or commonly result in higher recorded unemployment. The figures which do show large rises in these areas are those recorded for 'permanent sickness'.

It must be significant that the highest concentrations of people claiming Incapacity Benefit are to be found in the old industrial areas of the country. Half of the top 20 districts in the league table of sickness benefit claimants are former coalmining areas. In marked contrast, the bottom 10 areas in the same table are small town or rural districts in South-East England. Of the 68 districts with 10 per cent of the population out of work and claiming sickness related benefits, not one was in London, the South-East, South-West or Eastern England. Only 3 or 4 per cent of those of working age are sickness claimants in these areas, where jobs are relatively easy to come by.

Using as a benchmark the official sickness figure for the fully employed parts of the South and applying it to other areas where jobs are more scarce, Beatty and Fothergill assess that, nationally, a total of 1,130,000 people have been 'diverted' from unemployment to sickness benefits. They chart these diversions region by region. The highest figures in the table are for Scotland, Wales and Northern England, followed by the West and East Midlands. They are able to confirm the validity of their calculations by cross-checking with 1981 sickness levels in the various areas and with the proportion of Incapacity Benefit claimants who say they would like full-time jobs.

The authors of this study emphasise that there is nothing fraudulent about the conduct of those who claim Incapacity Benefit. Claimants have to be medically examined and certified either by their own doctors or, increasingly, those employed by the Benefits Agency. But this does not necessarily mean they are incapable of any kind of work It is simply that, where jobs are short, they are likely to find themselves at the end of a very long queue behind fitter and younger people.

The study concludes that the regional imbalances in the labour market are far more severe than is generally recognised. It is no good relying on the hope that this is a problem which will gradually disappear as those on Incapacity Benefit reach retirement age and move over to state pension provision. Unless this problem is recognised and tackled vigorously there will be no jobs for the young people growing up in these deprived areas. The dismal consequences of neglect are already to be witnessed in some of the old mining communities where lethargy, lawlessness and drugs are all too prevalent.

Beatty and Fothergill conclude with a plea for an effective regional economic policy which will multiply jobs in the places where they are needed. But New Labour believes fervently that the market is capable of producing solutions to all problems and eschews public intervention in the economy as likely to be ineffective or even harmful. Can even as powerful a case as has been presented here bring about a change of heart and mind?

Ken Fleet

Hope for Africa?

Basil Davidson, *The African Genius*, James Currey & Ohio University Press, 367 pages, paperback ISBN 085255799X £15.95

In the midst of African disasters in the Sudan, in Ethiopia and Côte d'Ivoire, and after those in Algeria, Ruanda and Sierra Leone, it was a bold act of James

Currey and the University of Ohio to think of republishing Basil Davidson's *The Africans*, and doing so under the new title of *The African Genius*. Davidson's *The Africans* appeared as a great work of historical scholarship in the 1960s, and can be said to have inspired a whole series of local and regional African studies that followed. For almost the first time since the African continent was divided up into fifty or more colonies of the European powers, taking no account of ethnic and language groupings, the history of the African peoples which Europeans had for long sought to deny, emerged, thanks to Davidson's studies, into the daylight of common knowledge. The profundity of that earlier ignorance appeared in the belief, continuing into the 1960s, that the walls of Great Zimbabwe must have been built by the Portuguese or, earlier, by the Phoenicians, or even the Queen of Sheba, anything but the possibility of black people.

What *The Africans* revealed was the extraordinary success of hundreds, even thousands, of different peoples in turning an inhospitable continent of deserts, savannah and tropical jungle into a home to live in and bring up new generations – from 2 or 3 million population at the beginning of the millennium to 150 million by the colonial period, and this despite the loss of some 12 million young men and women in the slave trade. Davidson's studies of a wide range of African peoples from many parts of the continent reveal common themes – of establishing a balance with nature and a moral order among communities. Nowhere in other civilisations has Aristotle's warning against excess and advocacy of moderation in all things been so carefully and so necessarily adhered to. African history saw the rise of kings and empires and the outbreak of wars and violence, but there were built-in social and moral resistances to these becoming self-destructive – until today.

Davidson's studies end with a note on the African resistance movements to colonial rule, and his own participation in that resistance, and with a word of warning about the future. Colonial rule destroyed much of the deep strength of African society, just as industrialisation had done in European society, but it had not supplied anything capable of replacing what was destroyed. The nation state, as Davidson makes clear in a later book, was the 'black man's burden' – 53 statelets in all Africa, some of less than a million people, providing the basis for the wealth and power of small élites dependent on the European trade for rewarding the clienteles that served them, at the expense of the mass of the working population. It was a terrible inheritance made worse by the declining importance today of Africa's staple products, except for oil. Famines have become endemic and violence has followed. Davidson's conclusion was, however, an optimistic one for the future. Africans have succeeded in adapting to change many times before. They can do it again, but they should be left alone and not have other patterns of civilisation imposed upon them. But that was forty years ago, and the epidemic of AIDS combined with increasing militarisation, as the Great Powers once again scramble to control Africa's resources, suggest a less hopeful outlook today.

Michael Barratt Brown